THE
IMPOSTOR
SYNDROME

PRAISE FOR
THE IMPOSTOR SYNDROME

I have worked with Harold Hillman for a number of years and he has offered honourable and wise counsel at all times. He is insightful, thoughtful and trustworthy. Harold's ideas on Impostor Syndrome are very true: many executives lack confidence and belief in themselves. Leadership has to be practical; it has to be about who you are, not some kind of theory. The ideas and the exercises in this book can help business people at all levels find their way by giving them the courage to admit their weaknesses so they can work on them and improve, and allowing them to take that final step into the space of a true leader.
— **Andrew Thorburn, CEO, Bank of New Zealand**

Harold helped us realise at Refining NZ that when we employ people for their thinking, we have to make sure they aren't pressured to moderate their views to fit 'what is acceptable around here'. I understand so much more now after reading *The Impostor Syndrome*. The linkage between authenticity and leadership is magical. I hope the book provides that eye-opening experience to others.
— **Ken Rivers, former CEO, Refining NZ**

In my experience far too many people are their own worst critics. Women especially are vulnerable to the limitations of self-doubt. We worry too much about presenting what others expect of us rather than allowing ourselves to trust our own skills, experience and judgement. Harold Hillman's book is a must-read for anyone who has experienced this feeling, but it especially resonates for me because it conveys the power of authenticity in a practical yet compelling way. If we have the courage as leaders to be ourselves, to show our vulnerabilities as well as our strengths, then Impostor Syndrome will not flourish in our organisations and people will have a much better chance to reach their true potential.
— **Barbara McKerrow, Chief Executive, New Plymouth District Council**

Be yourself — it sounds simple, so why do we make it hard, particularly in a business context? It takes insight and reflection to really know yourself, and courage to live and show the true you. We've all been impostors at some time, hiding our true selves. Harold demystifies Impostor Syndrome, showing us that it's okay and common to feel that way, but that the sooner we get over it and live authentically, the better off we and everyone around us will be. Read it and find yourself!
— **Alison Andrew, Executive Global Head, Chemicals, Orica**

I love this book! It is brilliant, timely and in a form that can be easily digested by anyone who wants to understand why authenticity makes a difference. The strategies to cope with Impostor Syndrome will resonate on so many levels and with a broad spectrum of readers. This is an important must-read book for anyone who is ready to take their leadership to the next level.
— **Graham Stuart, CEO, Sealord**

Amongst the plethora of books written on leadership, *The Impostor Syndrome* stands out as providing valuable insight into the essence and importance of an authentic approach along with a practical 'how-to' toolkit. For those looking to become a highly regarded and effective leader or eager to create an environment where authentic leaders can flourish, this book contains much to recommend it.
— **Chris Black, Chief Executive, FMG**

THE IMPOSTOR SYNDROME

BECOMING AN AUTHENTIC LEADER

HAROLD HILLMAN PhD

RANDOM HOUSE
NEW ZEALAND

RANDOM HOUSE

UK | USA | Canada | Ireland | Australia
India | New Zealand | South Africa | China

Random House is an imprint of the Penguin Random House group of companies, whose
addresses can be found at global.penguinrandomhouse.com.

Penguin
Random House
New Zealand

First published by Random House New Zealand, 2013
Text © Harold Hillman, 2013

The moral rights of the author have been asserted.

Design by Kate Barraclough and Kathleen Lonergan © Penguin Random House
New Zealand
Cover photograph: iStock/akurtz
Printed and bound in Australia by Griffin Press, an Accredited ISO AS/NZS 14001
Environmental Management Systems Printer

Photographs by iStock (pages 17, 30, 31, 39, 40, 41, 42, 43, 44, 89, 93, 94, 125 and 154)
and Shutterstock (pages 19, 97, 107, 117 and 120)

A catalogue record for this book is available from the National Library of New Zealand.

ISBN 978-1-77553-527-0
eISBN 978-1-77553-528-7

penguin.co.nz

DEDICATION

I know what it is like to feel like an impostor. I have lived that experience a few times in my life, during the early years and well into adulthood. My stories are your stories. All of our impostor stories give rise to a powerful insight about the importance of finding and being our authentic selves.

This book is written for anyone who is currently wearing the impostor's mask, and is dedicated to everyone in the world who has ever worried that being yourself is simply not good enough.

Above all else, always remember that there has only ever been, and will always only be, one you.

ABOUT THE AUTHOR

Harold Hillman is the managing director of Sigmoid Curve Consulting Group. The sigmoid curve is an algebraic formula that shows how growth and momentum are best sustained by disrupting the status quo. Hillman's personal and professional experiences exemplify the curve, which has been the catalyst for numerous adventures in his life's story.

Based in New Zealand since 2003 and a citizen since 2008, Hillman coaches business leaders and executive teams to appreciate the strong relationship between leadership and learning. He believes that the best leaders are also the most skilled learners.

Prior to Sigmoid, Hillman served in senior executive roles with Fonterra, Prudential Financial, and Amoco Corporation. Trained early in his career as a clinical psychologist, he moved in the direction of leadership and management development after serving on the faculty at the United States Air Force Academy.

Hillman earned his EdM from Harvard University and a PhD in clinical psychology from the University of Pittsburgh. An optimist who believes that change is a gift, Hillman lives every day through the prism of opportunity and possibility.

FOREWORD

All successful executives have employed their personal ambition to advance their careers and influence. By itself, ambition is a motivating emotion or a personal attribute. Ambitious people have a history of pushing themselves to their learning edge and taking on big challenges, knowing that the stakes are high, inadvertently setting up their experience of Impostor Syndrome.

'Ambition' is an interesting word. In Latin, the original verb was *ambire*, to go around a circuit, usually meant for soliciting favour or votes. A driving force was *ambition*, or a desire for something. The *ambitus* is the circuit, edge or periphery. A person who has ambition is driven by a personal desire to ask others to support her/his advancement.

When paired with avarice, ambition mutates into greed. Greed has been a part of recorded history since biblical times, and has thrived since the 1980s — the decade of greed. Peter Koestenbaum, published philosopher and mentor, explains that this avaricious expression of ambition 'feeds on other people, takes away in order to get, offends, breeds envy, and . . . leads to isolation from the world'. People seem to have a limited tolerance for unbridled greed, and eventually respond with policies and practices (including violence) to control such ambitious people. Unfortunately, significant if not irreparable damage has been done. This book isn't interested in this type of ambition.

Pair ambition with aspiration and greatness can happen. Servant leadership can emerge. Aspiration is the driving force behind a personal vision, a desire to create something good or better, a longing for perfection. Koestenbaum sees this strain of ambition as 'an ongoing dissatisfaction with what is and an insatiable appetite for realizing potentials that, by definition, can never be fulfilled'. Servant leaders envision a better future for their organisation, neighbourhood or society, and believe they can bring people and circumstances together to create that desired future. Servant leaders engage their own ambition to inspire and guide the collective aspiration of the people they serve. All are served well and benefit.

Ambition can be channelled by two governors: integrity and self-awareness. Integrity means adherence to a moral code or ethics. Moral codes are determined by families, tribes, religious groups, societies, or any social organising force, such as armies and gangs. If ambitious leaders believe they should not lie, cheat, steal or covet, their behaviours will be channelled away from those choices. If ambitious leaders believe 'the end result justifies the means', their behaviours will reflect a diversity of methodologies and techniques for achieving their goals regardless of collateral damage. Finding one's moral code requires deep reflection on lessons learned from others, difficult choices made in the course of becoming an adult, and strategies employed to advance in one's career. Being ethical requires knowing the lines of integrity that are firm, not to be crossed.

Self-awareness is the other governor on the expression of ambition. Knowing the essence of one's self — without the costumes of executive or politician or parent — is the foundation of making choices that align with one's ambition, i.e., who I want to become and what I believe I am capable of achieving. Having direct contact with one's inner private world of beliefs, thoughts, emotions, fears and hopes is the first step of self-awareness. It is a heightened understanding of one's self — the good, the bad and the ugly. It is where authenticity is rooted.

Harold Hillman and I met in the 1990s when he was chief learning officer for Amoco, a former oil company based in Chicago. He invited me to help design and deliver a development process to take Amoco's leadership to another level of complexity. My work was grounded in learning organisations with *The Fifth Discipline Fieldbook* series I co-authored with Peter Senge, Art Kleiner, Rick Ross and Bryan Smith.

I work with executive teams and boards of directors to build their capacity to think and act together in the best interest of the enterprise. The ability to perceive the foundation of one's own mental models, as well as be open to others' thinking and build a shared strategic model, are at the heart of my work.

I have collaborated with Harold on projects that have spanned the globe over the past 20 years. We have pushed each other to expand our models of leadership and personal mastery. We have coached each other to be better advisers on how to accelerate personal and team learning for our clients. We have laughed loudly, sent secret signals across a room, cried together and shared family time. I value Harold's professional perspective, which is built from his experience as a clinical psychologist, a business executive and an executive coach. You'll learn more about his character when you read the book. And you'll see why I cherish the time when we get to work together.

As Harold has done, leaders with aspirational ambition put themselves on the edge of their world time after time to learn and grow and achieve. Their dissatisfaction with reality generates their own discomfort by choosing to be in new and difficult situations about which they have limited knowledge. It is inevitable that they feel like an impostor for a period of time while they learn the new situation. When this happens, the challenge is how they — and you — respond to the temptation to be someone you're not, just to alleviate the pressures that come with navigating through uncertainty. You might argue that this is the ultimate challenge of life.

The purpose of this book is to offer clarity and strategy. Harold masterfully exposes the Impostor Syndrome, and you will see that he owns this territory, from both his personal and professional experience. When I read it, I breathed a sigh of recognition. I invite you to take the book home and get comfortable. As you read, reflect on how the profiles may relate to you and the people you know. Then consider how best to channel your aspirational ambition as you develop your capability to monitor your motivations, intentions and desired outcomes in real time, all the while remaining true to yourself and your vision.

Charlotte Roberts
Co-author of *The Fifth Discipline Fieldbook* and *The Dance of Change*

Contents

1.

Where does the term 'Impostor Syndrome' come from?

Impostor Syndrome, sometimes called 'Impostor Phenomenon' or 'Fraud Syndrome', is a term coined first in 1978 by two American psychologists, Pauline Clance and Suzanne Imes. It is a psychological phenomenon in which people — often facing a new or big challenge — are unable to internalise their accomplishments, attributing their success instead to luck, timing or some other external factor beyond their own making. Despite a continual striving for excellence that usually results in success, these individuals believe that they have tricked others into thinking they are bright and that it is only a matter of time before someone 'outs' them as frauds. Impostors experience terror when they think of failing at some goal that they set for themselves, and they take drastic measures not to make a mistake or lose the respect of others.

2.

What is Impostor Syndrome all about?

Beyond the research of Clance and Imes in the 1970s and a few studies and articles in the popular press in the 1980s, there has been little empirical research on the incidence and prevalence of Impostor Syndrome. We do know that it is neither an official clinical disorder nor a psychological disorder. It is fairly common and is situational — experienced by up to 75 per cent of all individuals at some point in life — although most people who are burdened by the symptoms don't know this, have no idea how to describe what they are feeling, and prefer not to talk about it.

There is a common misconception that 'no one else can possibly feel this way', which reinforces the need to stay quiet about it. Impostor Syndrome creeps into the psyche of the newly appointed captain of the football team, the newest member of the debate team, a first-time mother holding her baby, the successful applicant to the Harvard MBA programme, the recently appointed assistant professor who will teach that same programme, the surgical resident assisting with her first open-heart operation, the salesperson of the year being celebrated at the AGM, and even the incoming CEO who won the role over two widely respected internal candidates.

The syndrome is impervious to nationality, ethnicity, religion, social strata and gender, although there is evidence that it may be especially problematic for women. In the business world, female CEOs are still newsworthy and are likely to believe that their performance is being watched and assessed more closely than that of their male counterparts, and also that their performance reflects directly on women in general. Regardless of demographics, we do know that the syndrome is partial to people who impose pressure on themselves to be perfect, thereby limiting themselves by their unwillingness to learn, and by missing opportunities to be genuine and authentic people.

3.

The focus of this book

Impostor Syndrome is a big topic which can cover a vast domain. In this book, our focus will be primarily on the business world and how employees and managers at all levels often struggle to find the defining line between being themselves and being who they believe others want them to be. Sadly, many end up choosing the latter.

I hope the book generates good dialogue and debate about how authentic leadership can and does make a difference, both to individuals and to organisations. It is important that Impostor Syndrome be normalised, as an important first step to diminishing its potency. Executives, managers and boards can play a key role in this, by learning and modelling behaviour that counters the syndrome, and by creating a positive and open environment where there is no need for people to feel like impostors. Organisations that create the conditions for authentic leadership to thrive, can then make it easier for all employees to bring the 'whole person' to work.

4.

Unplugged

The beautiful thing about aspiration is that it typically comes with some aspect of a higher standard — wanting to be more, to give more, to have greater impact. For many of us, a big source of our pride and sense of contribution and self-worth stems from a history of being 'mostly' right about how life works. And being mostly right most of the time perpetuates the need for a higher bar — a higher standard that is typically self-imposed and brutal in its judgement of oneself if you dare to disappoint.

Life presents you with many dichotomies that fit nicely on horizontal continuums. The vast space that sits between perfection and degrees of imperfection is one of those dichotomies you can likely relate to. At the extremes on this particular continuum, absolute perfection and unalloyed imperfection are dangerous places to live indefinitely. They are best regarded as stakes in the ground that can give you some bearing on the wide space that serves as a bridge between the two extremes, where there is room to appreciate the benefits of both. The need for perfection turns your focus to high standards, quality and consistency — a rigour associated with delivering something or presenting yourself in a way that reflects extreme pride and ownership of the outcome. And being at peace with imperfection brings you a sense of comfort with vulnerability — that space in your head where seconds can seem like minutes, when you are waiting to see if people still think you are cool, still respect you, even though you didn't get it right this time.

It is in the space between perfection and complete imperfection — on that bridge — where authenticity resides. And where exactly that point is between the two extremes is going to be different for any two people. It is a very personal space, full of self-appraisal, doubts, fears, concerns, hopes and dreams. And it's in this space that you can find your core persona — the one that is sometimes referred to as the 'unplugged' persona.

> **It is in the space between perfection and complete imperfection — on that bridge — where authenticity resides.**

An unplugged persona is just like that of the rock star analogy where there are no flash stage lights or voice synthesisers, and no chorus of background singers or flurry of dancers moving about at Mach speed with everything choreographed to the second. It's just you in front of the microphone, while behind you a sole guitarist and maybe someone on the keyboard plays a quiet melody. It's just you at the mike with no synthesisers to correct a pitchy note or cover for unforgotten words. But it really doesn't matter, because people are drawn to how raspy and, in some cases, how earthy your voice is, and they are far more focused on your words than they are on the tune.

When you are unplugged, the thing that most people remember about their time with you is how you were, not what you did. They remember their experience with you. They remember that you were confident, yet relaxed. You were assertive, yet conciliatory to better ideas. Your presence was undeniable, yet you never overshadowed others' contributions. You brought forward the best of many dichotomies in a way that positioned them as interdependent rather than mutually exclusive worlds. When you are unplugged, there are fewer either/ors and a whole lot less of the harsh judgement you impose on yourself for not being perfect. Paradoxically, the sweet spot of authenticity — of being unplugged — is to realise that comfort with imperfection often begets a greater result. These are not mutually exclusive extremes.

And then with the *ding* of an incoming email or the vibrating mobile phone alerting you to yet another text message, you are called back to the demands of the real world. *Try being unplugged on your own time, buddy. The company, and particularly the boss and the team, are counting on perfection . . . on being right, not 'mostly right', every single time. A little bit of flash lighting won't hurt you, the synthesiser might smooth out a couple of those rough edges, and the background chorus can cover up for glaring mistakes. And whatever you do, get it right this time. And just in case you weren't aware, the world is watching.*

Enter Impostor Syndrome, stage left. It kicks in with a fervour that is teeming with anxiety, apprehension, self-doubt and pessimism, all swirling around in your head and causing you to be completely self-absorbed. It is hard for you to focus your attention outward when all these crazy thoughts are prodding you toward the extreme and making you cringe at the thought of bringing forward anything short of perfection. You can't be open, because that will expose potential flaws in your thinking. You can't profess your lack of expertise in anything, because that will render your voice less significant with your peers, or even your own team. And you don't take kindly to others probing you with questions when you are not quite sure how your answers will be judged or possibly used against you.

There are two things that are intriguing about Impostor Syndrome. The first is: the syndrome is largely self-imposed. Over time you find yourself listening more and more to an inner Critic, a voice that resides somewhere on that continuum between perfection and disaster. And that voice is typically far more critical, far tougher, than any boss might ever be with you. That inner Critic warns you that you are going to make a fool of yourself if you don't get it right. The inner Critic's booming voice warns you that, unless your solution is air-tight, others are going to soon discover you are a fraud.

The second thing that is intriguing about Impostor Syndrome is that it tends to strike those who have been asked to step up to take on a bigger role, perhaps where the decisions have far more influence and impact on the organisation and on overall results. But perhaps that's not so intriguing after all. Success breeds success in a virtuous cycle that can, over time and with several promotions, turn vicious. This cycle can entrap senior executives in a bubble that reinforces the need to be right, to never be wrong, and to be omnipotent. To be all-knowing and all-powerful is a mighty tall task to pull off. But your CV tells us you are up for the challenge. There is absolutely no room for a vulnerable moment in the world of an impostor. No room whatsoever.

A huge number of people who wear the title of 'leader' have experienced Impostor Syndrome at points in their career, most often following a promotion or when newly assigned to a role. Often this is amplified if you are new to a company and in a role where no one internal was deemed suitable or qualified to take it on. Or it may be that you have been with the company for a while and are in the same role, but you are now on a new learning curve with a major deliverable and it suddenly feels like a new job. It may be that you didn't ask for the role, but someone more senior has deemed you the best person to help the company work its way out of a situation. Or you just may be the only person around the table who reminds you of . . . you. Sometimes being the only one who looks or thinks differently, or simply *is* different from the others, increases the pressure to be perfect.

Your own thinking may be getting in the way of others seeing you as a truly authentic person.

Like most ailments, treating the symptoms will bring only temporary relief, enough to get you over a hurdle or two, but you know from experience that the symptoms will return at the next big challenge, where once again you will have to put on the mask of perfection. Like most ailments, treating the root cause may take longer, but it breaks the cycle and leaves you confident that you are not going to be knocked back at the next major hurdle. In the case of Impostor Syndrome, the real cure comes about when you are able to concede that your own thinking — your own thought patterns — may be working against the positive impact you could be having as a leader. Your own thinking may be getting in the way of others seeing you as a truly authentic person.

This book is written to appeal to each individual reader. As much as possible, I leave out the proverbial 'we' and talk instead to the definitive 'you'. Over years of coaching hundreds of leaders about Impostor Syndrome, I have had so many people exclaim: 'So that's what it's called!' Yes, it has a name. No, you are not alone. No, you are not going crazy. Yes, you can absolutely beat Impostor Syndrome.

In this book there are profiles of four people (a blend of real people and real scenarios) who have been on the emotional roller coaster caused by Impostor Syndrome. Chances are you will recognise elements of yourself in the profiles. You will probably also take note that their experiences aren't X-factor stories, but rather common experiences that you encounter in every day's challenge to be the best that you can be. Through others' experiences described in this book, and comparing those with your own, you will start to get good at diagnosing the symptoms of Impostor Syndrome, catching them earlier in the cycle, and often preventing them from taking hold. Finally, I will introduce some strategies that will enable you to treat Impostor Syndrome at its very core, removing a major impediment to you being your true authentic self.

As with any ailment, the symptoms are common enough to recognise. What makes the difference is the treatment, and that is where you come in. The cure comes from *within* rather than beyond you. There is no magic pill or injection. There is no brain transplant. In the great majority of cases, there is no need for a psychotherapist. The cure comes from within. And you most definitely are the one to make that happen. Unplugged.

5.

Your fingerprint

By virtue of your fingerprints, you are unique — the only 'you' in the world. Even identical twins have different fingerprints, shaped by their respective experiences in the womb. No one anywhere else on the planet, at any time in history, has lived the exact same life that you have. This means that you can really differentiate yourself on the basis of what makes you unique. Whereas an impostor spends a lot of energy trying to minimise or contain that uniqueness, you will find that your search for authenticity will have the opposite effect. Being yourself will enable you to give more of yourself, which is far more energising than living life behind a mask.

Just like a fingerprint, your authenticity is a phenotype — meaning that your uniqueness is determined by the interaction of your genes and your life's experiences. And, just like a fingerprint, the whorls and ridges of your authenticity are uniquely patterned, from the perimeter to the core of your very being. Everything about you, from the outside in, has the potential to be a genuine reflection of who you are, who you are not, and what you are about.

6.

My fingerprint

I grew up gay at a time when it wasn't cool to be gay, or at least it seemed that way to me . . . and to others like me, whom I later learned had also concluded the same thing. So I spent the greater part of my young life aspiring to be straight, as that seemed to nullify the anxiety in others, and most certainly in myself. To remove all doubts of myself as an impostor, I compensated by getting married, having children and joining the military. After all, it's hard to be gay if you are a husband, a father and a military officer! To fit in and be accepted — and acceptable — I often reached for the impostor's mask without even thinking about it. Wearing the mask helped make the noise and vulnerability go away; at least it did in the short term.

I wasn't prepared for Impostor Syndrome when I went to university. I had grown up in a low-income, African-American neighbourhood in Washington DC, where, while education was valued and encouraged by my parents, this wasn't the norm for many around me, especially in the late 1960s and early 1970s when gangs and violence became prevalent. I went to university at a small liberal arts college in Pennsylvania, four hours — and what seemed like another planet — away from home. As one of only five African-American students at Muhlenberg College in 1973, I hadn't anticipated what it would be like to be on display. My guidance counsellor, the only black staff member at Muhlenberg, advised me and the other four black students to study hard and do exceptionally well. She told us we were helping to break stereotypes about black students not being able to cut it at white universities. For four years, I studied hard and got good grades, but I'm not sure how much fun I really had. It felt like I had a whole race of people counting on me to do well.

And then there was Harvard University. In my junior year at Muhlenberg, my academic adviser helped me consider the choices among graduate school programmes I would eventually apply to. He suggested I consider Harvard. I told him 'no way'. But he encouraged me to give it a go, and so I did. And when I was accepted at the Harvard Graduate School of Education, that was the first time I really felt Impostor Syndrome kick in at maximum speed, in fifth gear on full throttle! I told myself that I couldn't possibly compete with kids who had come from more privileged backgrounds, whose parents and families had grown up in Ivy League circles. I was just a poor kid from the housing projects of DC. What could I possibly do at Harvard? It would be just a matter of time before they realised their mistake. Somehow they had let an impostor slip through the admissions process. A year later, I earned my master's degree with distinction from Harvard. The problem was, though, I hadn't enjoyed the experience: I had been too afraid that I would eventually be 'outed' as the kid who didn't really belong there.

While in the military, I was honoured to be sent as one of the US Air Force Academy's officers to participate in the now-famous 'Don't Ask, Don't Tell' commission, ordered by the Clinton Administration to overturn discriminatory policies against gays serving in the military. The problem was that at the time it was still illegal to be gay in the military. So the honour of being selected to serve on this distinguished panel was negated by the fact that I was wearing an impostor's mask during the entire ordeal. I listened to dozens of hours of testimony by military experts and senior brass who said the most disparaging and despicable things about gay people. And there I sat at the table with these bigots, nodding vigorously to their every word and praying like hell no one would discover the real truth about me. I was there because of my distinguished service as an officer, but I would have been dishonourably discharged had I chosen to speak from the experience of a gay person serving in the military. Like most impostors, I sat on my hands.

Later, at Amoco Corporation in Chicago, a very senior African-American executive whom I considered a mentor gave me some advice when I joined the oil giant after leaving the military. He told me that the best way to succeed in the corporate world was to emulate those at the very top of the company, none of whom reminded me of me. To make the point, he suggested that being seen as 'too ethnic' would work against black managers who aspired to rise in rank. I had never considered myself 'ethnic', much less 'too ethnic'. I took it as code for 'be white'.

Integrity got the best of me later in life, years after I began to grow weary of having to be the smartest and the straightest and the whitest person in the room. I didn't know what to call it at the time, but I realised I had spent the majority of my life as a compartmentalised person — only able to show glimpses of my true self when I felt very safe. The beautiful thing about integrity is that you are inclined to bring the multi-faceted dimensions of your whole self into one single person, taking away the need to be different people to fit different circumstances. But, while liberating and transformative, this revelation of integrity meant I had to make some difficult choices, none of which I regret decades later. It was Art Ryan, former CEO of Prudential Financial, who once told me: 'If you can't bring your whole self to work every day, we don't get the best from you.' That brief conversation was not only a defining moment in my life, it signified how important coaching by senior managers can be for younger managers who are trying to find their true, authentic selves.

As it turned out, Impostor Syndrome wasn't completely done with me, as I would have another bout in my transition to New Zealand. Being on a learning curve, not to mention several at one time, made conditions ripe and fertile for me to, once again, don the impostor's

The beautiful thing about integrity is that you are inclined to bring the multi-faceted dimensions of your whole self into one single person.

mask. New country and culture, new company, new sector, new challenges . . . all very exciting and daunting. And on top of it all, I would be joining the executive team, sitting with iconic giants in the industry, most of whom had more executive experience than me. What I didn't anticipate at the time, but soon came to know, was that we would all be navigating through new territory, trying to find our way, living with the vulnerability associated with leading the nation's largest business.

I tell aspects of my own journey to convey my deep and personal experience with Impostor Syndrome. Everyone will have different stories, but all can relate to the experience of being in 'stretch' or transition, moving from one set of challenges to even bigger expectations, many of which we impose on ourselves. The chapters in my life's story have brought me to a place of authenticity — where I'm okay with who I am, and who I am not. And perhaps the biggest revelation of all was to discover that what I considered a big deal wasn't a big deal for others at all. For years, I spent most of my time running away from what made me unique. I am proud to say that I no longer feel inclined to wipe away my fingerprint, as I am the only me on Earth.

'The privilege of a lifetime is to become who you truly are.'
C.G. JUNG, FOUNDER OF ANALYTICAL PSYCHOLOGY

7.

Inner voices

There are two inner voices that speak to you throughout the course of the day, every day. These two voices have grown up with you, so they know you well. This isn't like multiple personality disorder where you have alternate personalities that take over the main persona. And this isn't like psychosis where you have lost touch with reality and are experiencing hallucinations. These two voices are real and are grounded in your life's experiences. These two voices not only grew up with you, they grew up with each other. And although others can't hear them like you can, the evidence of their impact on how others experience you is undeniable.

THE CRITIC

One of those voices belongs to the Critic. The Critic cares about you with intense tenacity, and its foremost concern is that you don't let yourself or others down. *To whom much is given, much is expected.* It's a biblical passage that carries a lot of weight in the mind of someone who feels the need to not only succeed, but to succeed big. Quite often, not failing is more important to the Critic than succeeding big. Letting yourself and others down is a painful and lonely ordeal which only fortifies the power of the Critic's voice.

The Critic is the guardian of standards and order . . . with little tolerance for ambiguity or the grey areas of being.

The Critic's voice became dominant early in your life, sounding eerily like your parents or other important people who spent an inordinate amount of their time imposing standards and constraints on how you should be. As you began to shape your own distinctions between good and bad, right and wrong, perfect and imperfect, the Critic's voice became more distinct and adamant at critical decision points on your early learning curve. *Should I take the cookie? Should I return the cookie? Did I study enough tonight? Is doing poorly on tomorrow's exam the price to pay for an extra hour of sleep? You're not as good as Ted, so how did you get a spot on the team and he didn't? I can't believe they nominated me for class president — what do I know about leading anything? I'll never get into that programme at such a prestigious university. But I did. What did they miss?*

The Critic is the guardian of standards and order and all that is right, with little tolerance for ambiguity or the grey areas of being. The Critic refutes those who say you should be happy with your body as long as you are not morbidly obese. *A few grams are just a few grams, right?* For the Critic, relativity is a slippery slope that enables you to justify an extra gram or two, knowing you are moving further away from what the norms tell you is 'right'. The Critic keeps you awake questioning you about how you could possibly feel okay about a B+, a whole grade short of excellence. *Why didn't I go in and fight for an A on that paper? Why was I so relieved to see a B+?* The + is there to soften the blow and help justify how you could have missed the gold standard of excellence by just the smallest margin. That margin is akin to the difference between the few minutes the Critic allows you to relish a sweet victory before forcing you to obsess about what might have been.

You might say that the Critic is the Chief Justice of your soul's judiciary branch, also known as your conscience. Your conscience is there as an internal compass, helping you navigate the ethical and moral journey through life that ultimately builds character and defines who you are as a person. The Critic breaks the tie on votes that have the potential to redefine the bar — the gold standard — and rarely, if ever, does the Critic vote to lower the bar. *You didn't answer those questions clearly enough at this morning's board meeting. It doesn't matter that they agreed to invest in the project: you weren't at your best, and trying to justify your performance based on their vote lowers the bar for the next time.* Because the Critic prefers to see the world as black or white, grey is a bad colour where excuses tend to reside. And at its extreme, no excuse is good enough for your soul's Chief Justice.

Whatever you do, don't ever doubt that the Critic loves you. In fact, the Critic's major objective in your life is to keep you safe from harm. The fewer risks you take, the less you put yourself out there, the less you expose yourself to scrutiny and criticism, the safer you are. Perfection can't be disturbed in a safe protective bubble where there is minimal chance for error. That is how the Critic defines love.

THE COACH

The other voice belongs to the Coach. The Coach also loves you, but in a different way. The Coach sees taking risks as the fuel for personal stretch. The Coach believes that if you are too comfortable in a protective bubble, there is no opportunity to disrupt the status quo. And if you are locked into protecting the status quo that currently defines who you are as a person, it is very likely that you have no stretch, and ultimately no growth, in your life.

Personal stretch is attached to aspiration — not necessarily to be the best, but to be better than you currently are. Being the best puts you in a defensive position, warding off anything that could potentially unseat you. Being *better* than you currently are is a different mindset, one that keeps moving the goalposts, much like building a muscle. And while that may sound a lot like the Critic who raises the bar on performance, the big difference is that the Coach encourages you to risk failure in order to become stronger.

A young manager chose to face the pain and scorn of an angry group of employees who had been advised earlier in the week that their division was being sold to an undisclosed buyer and that the prospect of ongoing employment would be at the discretion of the buyer. While she was advised by HR to 'stick to the script' and avoid any impromptu questions, the manager chose to stay behind for an additional two hours to listen to the concerns and complaints of those affected by the decision. She was repeatedly shouted at and talked over, viewed by those in the crowd as the face of the corporate giant that couldn't give a damn. The manager was in murky waters, with no script to rely on, left to fend for herself, but the Coach told her to stay and make a difference. *You can't possibly walk out the door and not hear these people out. There are some things that you and the company can learn from this.*

The Coach understands that you grow to be resilient by facing adversity and failure, not by avoiding it.

This manager put her pride and reputation on the line — certainly at risk — and, while she knew it would be painful to stand in the line of fire at that moment, the Coach encouraged her to define for herself what was important, what she believed was the right thing to do for the employees. *What you are doing for these people will, in time, make a difference. And you need to take some of what you are learning back to your manager.* Making the decision to stay and face the angry group would help her develop her own resilience for future leadership challenges.

The Coach understands that you grow to be resilient by facing adversity and failure, not by avoiding it. The lead engineer on the team that designed the 'O' rings to seal the rocket boosters on the NASA space shuttle jeopardised his own reputation and career by constantly warning that there would eventually be a catastrophic accident related to broken seals on the rings. Whereas the Critic would have advised him not to risk the scrutiny and blame that would come in the aftermath of the shuttle *Challenger*'s explosion, the Coach would have been equally compelling in making the case for holding his own and taking that risk if he truly believed that lives were at stake.

History would eventually deem this engineer to be an ethical giant who set a new standard for business ethics and the sanctity of whistle-blowers, who more often decide to leave rather than fight the good fight. He became a better leader — a more resilient leader — by taking a big risk and walking through adversity on the strength of what he believed to be the right thing to do. The Coach would have been at his side every step of the way along that very personal journey.

The Coach helps you keep adversity in perspective, viewing it more as an opportunity to learn and grow rather than as a *fait accompli*. And there is a confidence that things will be okay on the other side of the challenge, the same as you feel on your first roller-coaster ride — an initial sense of dread and terror, followed by a surge of excitement and exhilaration when it was over. And for most of us, we are compelled to do it over and over again, because the Coach convinces us it will be okay. And it usually is.

ARE THE INNER VOICES HARD-WIRED?

It may feel as though the voices of the Critic and the Coach are hard-wired because they have been part of your thinking process for as long as you can remember. They are an inherent part of how you process and react to life's challenges and opportunities. The strongest empirical evidence which addresses the origin of your inner voices suggests that you were very likely influenced in early childhood by the outer voices of your primary caregivers. In most cases, your primary caregivers — the shapers of your thinking — were your parents and even your older siblings.

At the earliest age, years before peer influence takes hold, you become attuned to the norms, values and ethics that define the family unit. Mothers are especially influential on whether the Critic or the Coach is more prevalent in their children's heads. A self-critical six-year-old is most likely to become a self-critical adult. And chances are that the six-year-old is mirroring the thinking and behaviour of one or both parents or an older sibling. The same goes for a relaxed and laid-back six-year-old. Years later, you are likely to see the same demeanour on display, just more sophisticated in how it gets expressed.

Think about your own inner voices and how long they have been a part of your thinking process. And think about how closely your inner voices mirror those of your family unit, particularly one or both of your parents. This isn't due to genetics. The inner voices aren't hard-wired. How frequently you hear the Critic's or the Coach's voice — and your response to it — is learned. And that opens up a wonderful revelation for you.

The way you think has a direct impact on how you feel, which has a direct impact on what you do. The relationship between your thinking, feelings and behaviours is tightly linked. If the inner Critic tells you that you are unworthy to hold such a prestigious role, you are inclined to feel inferior and incapable, causing others to then experience you as tentative and withholding. If the inner Coach tells you to go for the new role because you can handle the stretch, you are inclined to feel excited and confident, causing others to then experience you as strong and vibrant.

On your quest to become an authentic leader, you will have to become more attuned to the presence and volume of both the Critic and the Coach. They operate in tandem and are responsible for how high you set the bar and how much risk you are willing to take to test yourself.

WHICH INNER VOICE IS MORE PREVALENT IN YOUR EAR?

SCENARIO 1

Your manager sent you a note earlier today asking if you would be willing to stand in for him to serve as an expert panellist at a national business conference in two weeks' time. The conference attendees include top business leaders from around the country, including two members of your board who had originally nominated your manager for the panel. Which inner voice is more prevalent in your ear?

THE CRITIC: Why is he asking you? Isn't Sam available? You're good, but hardly an expert. You couldn't possibly fill your manager's shoes, and everybody is probably going to be disappointed with you as a substitute, especially the two directors. But you know you can't say no. Well, you better cancel most of your meetings next week so you can get yourself prepared.

THE COACH: This is awesome! You need to hop onto this right away and see what you have to do to get prepared. Call the two directors and ask their advice on how you should best position your expertise, and see what ideas your manager has from his prep materials. This will be a great opportunity.

SCENARIO 2

Your company is going through a cost-reduction initiative and the chief financial officer (CFO) has requested that you serve on the project team that will make final budgetary recommendations for the coming year. The project team consists of six members, all of whom are more senior than you. So you are really surprised when the CFO asks you to be the major liaison person with the external firm that will shape the process. You are also aware that the project team is not popular among the business unit leaders. Which inner voice is more prevalent in your ear?

THE CRITIC: Being on this project is, almost without fail, the kiss of death for anybody associated with it. Look at what happened to Sandra two years ago when she led the process, the same as they are asking you to do now. She didn't see it coming, but several business unit leaders never forgave her for the cuts they had to make. Do you want to be marginalised like she was? Maybe you should reconsider.

THE COACH: Two years ago, you made some recommendations to Sandra about how the process she designed might have gained more support. Now you get your chance to show that it can, which is probably why you have been asked to design it this time. The first thing you will want to do is shape the message, so set up some meetings with key business leaders to make sure they have got proper context.

SCENARIO 3

You asked two friends to read a short story that you have written, and both of them have come back with rave reviews, insisting that you submit your story to a competition sponsored by a prestigious writers' society. Three of the judges are prominent authors, the fourth an Oxford scholar. You have dabbled with writing all your life, but this is the first time you have ever considered putting it all out there for the world to see. The submission deadline is in two weeks' time. Which inner voice is more prevalent in your ear?

THE CRITIC: Aw, come on now! Be reasonable. You're good; you know that. But a prestigious competition like this? No way are they going to take your story seriously. Think of how you are going to feel when you get that rejection letter. Don't put yourself out there like that. And you've got too many other things on right now — you can't possibly meet that deadline, can you?

THE COACH: You never saw this coming as quickly as it has. It's a pretty cool feeling to see how things are moving along. You should give it a real shot here. You can make some time this weekend and next week to make some revisions. What do you have to lose? The worst that can happen is a rejection letter. Hell, hang it in a frame and have a few good laughs!

If your inner voice sounds more like the Critic, you are more inclined to feel vulnerable in situations that directly test your competence or capability. If your inner voice sounds more like the Coach, you are probably more comfortable with taking risks, even if you still fear that others will see you as imperfect. The symptoms of Impostor Syndrome are more likely to surface when the Critic is most prevalent in your ear. However, the Coach can also take you into some vulnerable zones where you may be inclined to reach for the impostor's mask.

8.

··

Impostor Syndrome: What are the symptoms?

Like any disease outbreak, there are typical conditions that make it likely for the symptoms of Impostor Syndrome to surface. The one condition that is common across all impostor profiles is the heightened sense of vulnerability that a person feels. We will spend time later defining and exploring vulnerability, but let's give it a short definition here. Vulnerability is the sense of wandering into territory where you are no longer in total control of how things unfold. That can be the decision to take a new co-worker into your confidence, or being asked — with no notice — to speak on your team's behalf, or standing up to give the most important presentation of your career.

Like a baby contemplating her first steps, vulnerability is both enticing and frightening. The Coach wants to push you into that territory of uncertainty. The Critic warns you of the ramifications should you decide to venture there. There is a natural inclination to protect yourself should you decide to take those steps forward, giving up some or all control. The degree to which you feel the need to regain control will determine the magnitude of the symptom profile. The eight symptoms described here are most likely to surface when you loosen the grip on certainty. See how many of them you can relate to.

THE SYMPTOMS

GUARDED AND DEFENSIVE

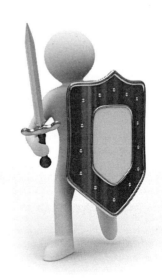

- Overly sensitive to small criticisms or suggestions for improvement
- Views critique as a personal attack
- Tends to present ideas or suggestions as edicts rather than matters for consideration
- Closed to incoming data that warrant another look
- Withholding or slow to divulge information or position
- Lacks transparency

- Treats information as power
- Views inquiry as a threat
- Lacks spontaneity and the ability to 'trust the flow'
- Unlikely to reveal or acknowledge mistakes or shortcomings
- Skilled at deflecting focus away from self and onto others

A guarded and defensive person seems closed and hard to penetrate. Getting information or a view from this person is like pulling teeth. The vibe you get is 'stay away' or 'stay out of my space'. This person is likely to be on-edge and become aggressive at the slightest provocation, and they don't appreciate it when you ask too many questions. This person is not going to open the proverbial kimono.

CALCULATING

- Focused more on what is probable rather than what is possible
- Overly focused on the sequence and granular details of next steps
- Often invests more energy into planning rather than execution
- Unlikely to deviate from a plan, even when spontaneity is better suited to the situation
- Analysis is often used as a brake on momentum
- Unlikely to lead from the front; more inclined to speculate from the rear

A calculating person tends to come across as sceptical or doubting, in what might be described as a halting energy, even in the most optimal circumstances. The focus is more likely to be on what might go wrong rather than on what will work well. This person is unwilling to deviate from process, even if spontaneity or innovation may result in a quicker or better outcome. To use a driving analogy, this person is the type who prefers to brake rather than accelerate.

COMPARTMENTALISED

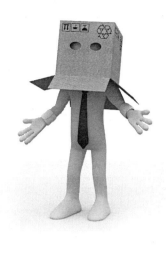

- Tends to be 'buttoned down' and corporate
- Unlikely or unwilling to disclose about their personal life
- Seemingly uninterested in the personal lives of others
- Not good at small-talk; more inclined to jump right in
- Considers meetings are about work, not opportunities for social networking
- Avoids social activities with colleagues outside the workplace
- Draws a firm distinction between work and play
- One person at work, another person outside work

A compartmentalised person seems to become a corporate robot when walking through the workplace door, speaking and dressing the part, unwilling to be flexible in style or approach. Getting things done takes priority over having fun, so others are likely to see this person as stuffy or uptight. This person is most comfortable when focused on work, not on more holistic matters. Yet you catch glimpses, or hear from others, that this person is a different beast outside the workplace.

INVULNERABLE

- Struggles to acknowledge personal flaws or imperfection
- Struggles with people who are able to acknowledge personal flaws or imperfection
- Harsh with self after a mistake or misstep
- Overly focused on the positive
- May blow little things out of proportion
- Impatient with others' mistakes
- Takes it personally if the team is not doing well

- May struggle with answering the question 'What would you do differently?'
- May come across as detached from, or in denial of, imperfect outcomes
- Difficult or unable to concede that another person's viewpoint is better than their own
- Saving face is more important than surfacing heated issues

An invulnerable person is likely to soak up all the praise when things go well and become the master of deflection when things go wrong. Personal accountability pertains only to success, not failure. This person finds it difficult to concede that another point of view or approach is better, almost as though saving face is the foremost objective. Concession is the single last resort to consider.

INFLEXIBLE

- Rigid with views, even when in consultation
- Tends to prefer 'but' over 'and'
- Looks for reasons to denounce an opposing view or opponent
- The need to be right tends to drive interactions with others
- Selects data and de-selects other data to prove self right
- Unwilling to explore assumptions behind a point of view that may be faulty
- Finds fault in the messenger in order to discount the message
- Views win–win as a suboptimal outcome
- Intolerant of divergent thinking; far more comfortable with convergent thinking

An inflexible person equates 'being right' with 'being an effective leader'. Consequently, there is a tendency to dig in and hold one's ground rather than to assume an open and objective posture about other possibilities. This person takes pride in being efficient and quick, both with analysis and decision-making. To ponder a view or give pause for reflection is viewed by this person as a weakness.

LITTLE OR NO HUMOUR

- Overly serious
- Never pokes fun at self
- Overly sensitive when others poke fun
- Seemingly uncomfortable to step out of character
- Skilled at deflecting focus away from self and back onto others
- Misses opportunities to energise a team or others with levity
- Tends to use humour as a weapon rather than an energiser

A person with little or no humour is a stuffed shirt, serious about everything and unable to find the slightest bit of humour or fun in anything. For this person to laugh or show some levity, the Earth is surely to open up with a huge devouring maw and swallow the business whole. And be careful about poking fun at this person — do so at your own peril. In short: this person is a buzz-kill.

COMPENSATING — OVER THE TOP

- Drawn to the spotlight and unlikely to relinquish it
- Overly bold and forceful with pronouncements
- Excessive focus on personal accomplishments and achievements
- Refers to previous company examples repeatedly
- Quick to cut off others or turn their words to support their own position
- Slick; a fast talker

COMPENSATING — BELOW THE PARAPET

- Avoids the spotlight and quickly refocuses it on others
- Reticent to state a view first; more likely to go last
- Projects a tentative voice and posture
- Assertions lack conviction or energy
- Tends to gravitate toward the majority view
- Sees standing alone as unsafe and unwise

Compensating symptoms can often take a person to one of two extremes. The over-the-top person is loud and brash, in heavy advocacy, and unlikely to yield the floor or the spotlight out of fear of being upstaged. The below-the-parapet person is quiet and unassuming, more likely to find a corner of the room to blend into a crowd, and is very uncomfortable when put on the spot to assert a view. You are likely to get one or the other compensating type in any given person.

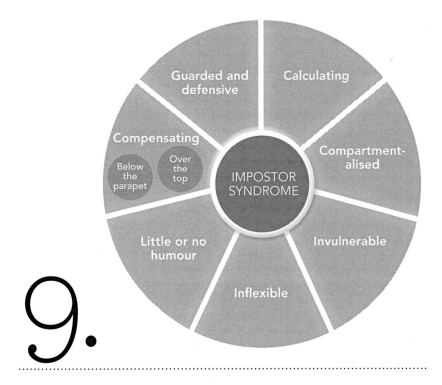

9.

What the symptoms of Impostor Syndrome tell us

You can see the potential interplay between the symptoms of Impostor Syndrome. At the core of them all, there is a sense of insecurity associated with being able to meet the expectations of others. And the funny thing about it is that, quite often, those expectations are not directly expressed by others, but instead are self-imposed. It is how you size up a challenge relative to your own perceived capability to meet it. There is a tendency to either inflate the challenge, where it becomes bigger than it actually is, or minimise your own capability to take it on. And when either or both of these factors are in play, your first line of defence is to reach for the impostor's mask.

An impostor is self-absorbed, more serious than fun, careful and cautious, constantly scanning for incoming threats, unlikely to acknowledge a shortcoming or a mistake, unwilling to yield to a better idea, and unable to relax and be 'in the moment'.

When you are an impostor, a big part of your energy is fear-based. You are hypersensitive to every little glance, whisper or innuendo. *Why is she looking at me like that? What are the two of them whispering about over in that corner? My presentation must have been awful; no one has come over to say they liked it.* When you are behind the impostor's mask, you are constantly looking for external validation that you have done a good job. Every raised eyebrow, every yawn, every nod of a head means something, and very often you will internalise these disparate and frivolous data as confirmation of your worst fear. *They have figured me out. I am not the person they think I am.*

When the symptoms are at full throttle, the fear and panic begin to rise, perpetuating a direct connection between what you are thinking and how you are feeling. You become a person in mental free-fall, spiralling with a dreadful sense that you are about to make a fool of yourself. When this happens, you are inclined to deflect attention and focus away from yourself. If you can get yourself out of the spotlight it gives you a chance to compose yourself and re-adjust the mask so that it is fitting as tightly as it can across your real persona. Impostors are masters of deflection.

An impostor is self-absorbed, more serious than fun, careful and cautious, constantly scanning for incoming threats, unlikely to acknowledge a shortcoming or a mistake, unwilling to yield to a better idea, and unable to relax and be 'in the moment'. Being an impostor is a full-time job that requires lots of energy. Being an impostor can bring you to the brink of exhaustion, and with time it wears you down. Few impostors have the stamina to sustain this drain on energy indefinitely.

Putting that mask on, day after day, year after year, takes a lot out of you. It is when you are standing alone late at night in front of the mirror, mask in your hand and to your side, that you see the vulnerable reflection of you staring back, wondering why you are making things so hard for yourself.

10.

Four profiles of Impostor Syndrome

You are about to meet four 'ordinary' people, who, despite their different backgrounds and experiences, have some key experiences in common. They each work for or run a business, have done well in their respective careers, and are confronting a prospective opportunity with dread and apprehension. And each of them is experiencing a full onslaught of Impostor Syndrome.

A.J. Rawlings is early in her career, still finding her way, when she gets an opportunity to represent her company at an industry conference. Michelle Stanson has just been promoted as a rising star in the executive ranks of a company that is counting on her to spark growth in the Asia Pacific region. Daniel Li is a new external hire who has been brought on board to join the leadership team, infuse a new way of thinking and shake things up. Peter Reilly's company is sending him to Brazil to fix a huge mess that could potentially cripple the business in their largest growth market. Big opportunities, big expectations, big fears . . . ideal elements for the perfect storm, also known as Impostor Syndrome.

As you read the four profiles, look for and imagine the interplay of symptoms from the previous pages. Imagine the voices of the Critic and the Coach as they whisper words of caution or encouragement. Put yourself in the shoes of these four people as they come to terms with the pressure to meet and exceed exorbitant expectations. And relate their profiles to your own life's experiences so that the connection you feel with each of them is real and visceral. When Impostor Syndrome is in full swing, it is a very daunting place to be, which makes it even tougher to talk about feelings and thoughts that nearly everyone around you can relate to. Which is really one of life's incredible paradoxes.

A.J. RAWLINGS
'SENIOR TEAM CO-ORDINATOR'

THE BACKGROUND

The moment A.J. put her bag down at the table and claimed her seat next to the neatly dressed woman in blue, she had a sinking feeling about how the morning would go. Four others soon joined the table, a full complement of six, as was the case at the other nine tables evenly placed around the large conference room. A.J. nervously scanned the room, and within seconds she had deduced that she was one of the youngest people there. Out of 60 or so delegates at this conference, she didn't like the feeling of standing out, especially as the youngest. Although A.J. hadn't given a whole lot of thought to who might be there, somehow this wasn't what she had been expecting. It was hard for her to put her finger on why she was feeling so nervous, but that was how she was feeling.

Three weeks earlier, A.J. had been anything but nervous when her boss, Cynthia, surprised her with the offer to attend the Conference Co-ordinator's Conference — or 'C3', as it was advertised in one of the larger trade journals. In fact, A.J. had been ecstatic over being asked to attend and represent Blue Ridge. Until the moment Cynthia asked her to attend C3, it hadn't even occurred to her that, although she spent most of her days organising conferences, she had never been a participant at one herself. A.J. had called her mother shortly after Cynthia told her about the conference. Her mother hadn't been supportive of her taking the job with Blue Ridge, and had predicted that she would not do well. 'You can hardly organise your own life,' her mother had said. 'What makes you think you can organise anything for other people? You're hopeless at that sort of stuff.' A.J. felt the need to prove her mother wrong, and that day she nearly gloated over the phone about how her company was sending her to this big conference. Although she hadn't anticipated her mother's response, she wasn't surprised when her mother replied, 'Oh, they found something wrong with you, did they?' This was a battle that A.J. just wasn't going to win.

At 24, A.J. was pretty proud of how her career and life were progressing. She had taken a lot of criticism from her mother and relatives when she had decided against going to university, opting instead to move to Timaru to live with an older cousin who encouraged her to learn about the world first and then focus on her studies. In her first two years away from home, A.J. held a myriad of jobs, ranging from working at the deli of the local supermarket to being a customer services rep for Vodafone in the heart of Timaru. She learned about the job at Blue Ridge Productions from a girlfriend who was the owner's cousin. They were looking for someone to help organise conferences and business meetings. A.J. had been intrigued by the job description, maybe because she had spent her life hearing others around her express dismay about her lack of order and structure. Her grandmother had affectionately referred to her as a 'human tornado'. Maybe this was part of the intrigue, A.J. had wondered at the time. She took the job and, nearly two years later, she loved everything about it. Being asked to attend the conference was the icing on an already delicious cake!

The day before the conference, Cynthia asked A.J. to use this as an opportunity to promote and market Blue Ridge, as a sizeable portion of their revenue was from sub-contracting to other conference planners. While Cynthia normally attended these types of trade conferences, she saw this as a step-up opportunity for A.J., both to learn about best practice in the field, and to build her professional network beyond Blue Ridge. Up until then, A.J. had largely played a background role in organising professional meetings, taking her lead from Cynthia or Jenny, one of the other more experienced team co-ordinators. Both Cynthia and Jenny wanted A.J. to grow, so they encouraged her to come back with lots of good ideas about how they might innovate their own business model. This was all very new turf for A.J., who was excited but a bit daunted. *It's one thing to attend the conference — it's another thing to bring something useful back.* She wouldn't have been able to describe then what she would one day look back on as the early twinges of Impostor Syndrome. *What are Cynthia and Jenny expecting me to come back with?*

THE SITUATION

Now seated at the front table with five other people, all of whom looked very experienced and sure of themselves, A.J. found herself focusing on the two-day agenda. 'Best practice' sessions were interspersed throughout the day, and delegates were encouraged to sign up for 'dialogue circles'. A.J. couldn't imagine that she had anything to share that these people would find even remotely close to best practice. She suddenly wondered why Cynthia or Jenny hadn't come to the C3 instead of sending her. *They would have been more at home here. They would be able to talk confidently about Blue Ridge.* And as the table introductions began, everybody standing to introduce themselves one by one, A.J. found her heart beating at an excessive rate, the first time in her life she had ever felt the need to hide.

Theirs was the fourth table to introduce themselves. A.J. had never heard so many fancy and important titles: managing director of this, CEO of that, co-founders and senior partners — even a couple of vice presidents. A.J. thought it sounded more like a political convention than a meeting for conference co-ordinators. The woman in blue turned out to be 'Heather Freeman, co-founder of Freeman Communications, runner-up in this year's national small business entrepreneur awards' — all said with an air of confidence that made A.J. feel even smaller. Turns out that Heather was also on a local government board, which she managed to mention without missing a beat as she took her seat. The room seemed very quiet as A.J. rose slowly from her chair. Never before had she been this nervous, this out of sorts. She felt absolutely exposed as she stood to tell the curious audience, all eyes trained on her, about why she deserved the right to be sitting here among such giants. *Why oh why isn't Cynthia here instead?*

'Hello everyone,' A.J. said meekly, clearing her throat. 'My name is Anna Rawlings.' *Anna Rawlings? Anna? You haven't called yourself 'Anna' since you could walk. You hate the name Anna. You've been 'A.J.' all your life, but you just told them your name is Anna. What's that all about? Does 'A.J.' sound too childish? Not grown-up enough? 'Anna' sounds more grown-up, does it?*

A.J. continued. 'I'm the . . . senior team co-ordinator with Blue Ridge Productions . . . we're based in Timaru.' *Senior team co-ordinator? Senior team co-ordinator? What the hell is that?* It had not occurred to A.J. until that very moment that she had never introduced herself formally to anyone. She didn't quite know what to call herself. All she knew was that it needed to sound as important as all the other fancy titles attached to all these important people, including Heather Freeman, who seemed to be looking at her now with increased scrutiny. A.J. fumbled her way through two or three more sentences about Blue Ridge, calling it a 'small company', then immediately correcting herself by saying, 'Well . . . we have 17 people on staff, so I guess that makes us not so small.' *Not so small? Not so small? You just described your company as 'not so small'. Nice going, A.J. — Cynthia would be real proud of you right about now, what with you being a 'senior team co-ordinator' and all that.*

A.J. never heard the other six tables full of important titles introduce themselves. They were all a blur in the background, drowned out by her own surge of doubt and insecurity, as she glanced again at the agenda and wondered what she could possibly contribute to some of these sessions. In fact she was so self-absorbed that she completely missed a delegate at the ninth table who said, while introducing herself, 'A special hello to you, Anna. I used to work with Jenny. Please give her my regards.' Heather tapped A.J. on her shoulder to get her attention. A.J. had not responded to the name 'Anna'. She didn't even realise the woman was addressing her, as it had been years since anyone had called her Anna. It was really awkward when she realised everyone was, once again, focused on her. She turned nervously toward the other table, smiling at no one in particular. Mercifully, the introductions were soon over.

The real fun was about to start, as each table learned that their first task was to brainstorm the most unconventional way to host a conference for conference co-ordinators. *Put the doctors to work, working on the doctor.* A.J. could feel Heather's energy swell as the woman in blue leapt to her feet to grab the marker on the flip chart. Heather was clearly in charge here. She wrote the words 'Brain Energy from Table Four' at the top of the page and then turned to the table and said, 'Let's go around first. Anna, we'll start with you. Do you have any thoughts about how we might tackle this wonderful challenge?' Anna Jo Rawlings looked back at Heather in dismay. She still couldn't believe she was answering to the name Anna. It was like she couldn't ground herself, probably like when a person has amnesia and is trying to figure out who they are. A.J. was trying to channel 'Anna' to come up with some 'brain energy' for Heather. For the third time in a very uncomfortable 15 minutes, all eyes were again trained on the 'senior team co-ordinator from the not-so-small company in Timaru'.

On the first break, Anna worked up the nerve to tell the woman who knew Jenny that 'my friends call me A.J.'. The woman smiled and said, 'A.J., huh? I like that.' Feeling more confident, A.J. tried out her new identity with two others before the break was over. No one winced at learning that her brand was two letters rather than a full name. At lunch, she sat with three other delegates, one of whom she had worked with in the morning's second breakout session. This guy, named Paul, told her he had grown up near Timaru and he was curious to learn more about Blue Ridge. As they talked, A.J. learned that Paul was new to the profession, having spent most of his young career working as a staff engineer at a construction firm. He had decided on his thirtieth birthday that he needed to do something radically different and so, one month after his birthday, he had joined a firm called The Big Tent, which A.J. had heard Cynthia talk about. Paul had been there for only seven months and his boss wanted him to come to this conference to learn the ropes and meet some new people.

Paul told A.J. that he felt 'pretty awesome being the "greenest" person in the room'. He said, 'It takes the pressure off me having to know everything. That's what I love about my new job — I'm learning something new every day.' Then Paul said to A.J., 'I forgot what you do with Blue Ridge. What's your position?' Four hours earlier, she had been 'Anna, the senior team co-ordinator'. Now A.J. said to Paul, with a laugh full of relief: 'I don't really have a title, Paul. We're too small to get hung up over that kind of stuff.' For the first time since taking her seat that morning, A.J. allowed herself to relax. And when she called Cynthia that afternoon to tell her how things were going, she no longer had regrets that her boss had sent her to C3.

A.J. had learned something new about herself that morning: that her mother's voice was more prominent in her head than she had imagined. She would have to pay more attention to that in the future. She had also learned that 24-year-old A.J. from Timaru, without the benefit of a university degree and with an inherent disorder to her life, could hold her own with all the fancy titles around her at C3.

A.J. had learned something new about herself that morning: that her mother's voice was more prominent in her head than she had imagined.

Little did A.J. know that those lessons would be tested with vigour less than 24 hours later, when, on the second day, her table selected her to play the CEO of a small company in a simulation where they had to compete with another group. Once again, A.J. felt a surge of panic, prompting her to think that the lessons from the day before were just the beginning rather than the end of something she was going through. Perhaps this was something she needed to go through . . . in order to grow.

WHAT SYMPTOMS OF IMPOSTOR SYNDROME DO YOU SEE IN A.J.?

Like many young people, A.J. wants to make her mark on the world in a way that enables her to grow and learn and have a sense of fulfilment. A.J. had never asserted herself in quite the fashion she had done when her mother insisted that she go to university. Given her sheltered upbringing, A.J. believed that working, rather than studying, would provide the better education. She felt she needed to land on something she could excel at, while still being true to her free spirit.

A.J. found it odd that people were very critical rather than affirming of her free spirit, which they translated as lacking structure and order in her life. Her mother and others predicted that her free spirit was going to be her biggest liability. However, while she wanted to prove those important people in her life wrong, she didn't want that to be her primary motivator. Impostors often find themselves motivated to prove others wrong, rather than strive for what may be personally fulfilling to them. A.J. was becoming more aware of this tension in herself.

The conference was the first time, perhaps since high school, that A.J. had been in a situation where she felt inadequate when comparing herself to others. Several of her school girlfriends had matured ahead of her; so she had been in this space before. But A.J. hadn't anticipated how confronting this would be in a professional setting. It took her off guard that she would immediately conclude that all these people were better qualified than she was. Why would she jump to such a drastic conclusion, particularly one that made her feel so nervous, so exposed? A.J. knew nothing about the internal Critic when that all happened. She would not have understood that one of the Critic's primary goals was to keep her safe, to make sure she was not exposed to criticism, just in case she really turned out to be the least experienced person in the room. Better safe than sorry.

This might explain why A.J. felt the need to hide — but why would she then start inventing a new identity as 'Anna'? And why would she make up some crazy fancy title — 'senior team co-ordinator' — that sounded absolutely absurd when she reflected later on the experience? And the need to inflate the size of Blue Ridge? They were a small company because they liked being a small company. Why did that suddenly matter to A.J.?

These are all legitimate questions to ponder when you feel the need to reach for the impostor's mask. When you are exposed to the scrutiny of others, there is a tendency to create a shield of armour around those things that make you feel most vulnerable. *Did I go to the right school? Do I belong to the right network? Have I worked for the right companies?* It is pretty common when people inflate their life's experiences to make themselves less susceptible to scrutiny or rejection. That's certainly what was going on for A.J.

Ironically, the very thing you are most worried about is the thing you often draw the most attention to. It's crazy the way an impostor's mind works. Most of us have certainly been there.

MICHELLE STANSON

NEWLY APPOINTED CHIEF OPERATING OFFICER

THE BACKGROUND

On the plane ride from San Francisco to Sydney to take on her role as chief operating officer of Nova Asia Pacific, Michelle Stanson found herself reflecting back on her fast-paced career . . . on her fast-paced life. This promotion and relocation had all happened so quickly that she hadn't really taken much time out over the past three months to do anything but focus on the new role. The 14-hour flight now provided her with some much-needed mental space to do some thinking about this next big chapter in her life. As the plane taxied on the runway awaiting permission to launch southward into a different hemisphere, Michelle settled into her seat and took some time to think.

No matter what the scenario happened to be, Michelle had always seemed to stand out for being ahead of the learning curve on some important metric. At her first paediatric appointment after birth, Michelle was projected in the ninetieth percentile for females likely to be at least six feet tall. She reached 5' 11" when she was 17 and that was it; but although that last inch had defied her, that was a rare event. Being born in the month of December meant that Michelle would normally have started school at the age of six rather than five, but her aptitude as a pre-schooler left no doubt that she would not only start early, but excel over most of her older peers. With a knack for learning, she became a verbal whizz-kid. At seven, Michelle began to read the dictionary. At nine, she became the youngest spelling bee champion in her school's history. And while she placed fifth in the regional face-off for the spelling bee champion, it was noted that Michelle was the youngest contestant ever to reach the semi-final rounds.

Michelle grew up quickly, almost like she was fast-tracking through her teen years, always focused on the next medal or award to compete for.

Often being the tallest and the youngest in any crowd, these extremes created interesting challenges for Michelle. As her school years progressed, she began to excel in sport as well, gaining a spot on the netball team where she became friends with the older girls. Michelle grew up quickly, almost like she was fast-tracking through her teen years, always focused on the next medal or award to compete for. It was only later, during her university years, that Michelle realised how little time she had actually spent enjoying those moments of glory. She came to realise that her energy surged not at the point of victory, but while anticipating it. The next challenge always seemed to interest her more than the victory at hand.

At university, Michelle excelled at commerce, but she was far more compelled toward information sciences courses. She had an aptitude for technology and design, enabling her to use her love of the written word when helping other students, and even some instructors, with various projects. Despite five offers to join prestigious companies with huge brands, very few people were really surprised when Michelle accepted a graduate-level entry role with a smaller global IS company with corporate offices in the heart of California's technology corridor.

Within her first year, Michelle had defined herself as exceptional, seen by her managers as having raw capacity and the aptitude to master a learning curve quickly. She also gained a reputation for learning as much as she could about the company's structure and portfolio, wanting to become as literate as possible about how the matrixed organisation worked.

At the annual talent review led by the executive team two years after Michelle joined, she was the most junior of 10 high-potential employees selected for the accelerated development programme. As Michelle had come to expect by now, her life was moving from one 'fast track' to the next, each raising her visibility as well as the expectations of others that she would do well. Sometimes Michelle wondered what others saw in her that she couldn't quite see. While she was flattered by her continued success and the confidence others had in her, there was also a part of her that worried silently about disappointing her supporters, very much the same way she had often worried about disappointing her parents at the spelling bees. But she never breathed a word of this to anyone.

The accelerated development programme paired Michelle with a senior executive who ran the company's innovation pipeline. Kelvin Stuart had been with Nova since its inception, having brought with him rich experience from Microsoft. Kelvin liked nurturing and stretching high-potential talent and he took an instant liking to Michelle, and the respect between them was mutual. Over the next four years, as Michelle rotated between assignments, including an eight-month role as an analyst on a joint venture project team, she listened closely to Kelvin's coaching. He advised her to think foremost about her brand and reputation as a leader, not as a technical expert. While it would take several more years for Michelle to fully appreciate the distinction Kelvin was trying to make, she got the gist of what he was saying. *Do whatever you can to position yourself as a shaper of the bigger picture, not the details. Let them know that your brain thinks in terms of possibilities. Keep one step ahead of everybody else. That's what fast-trackers do.*

After six years with Nova, at the age of 27, Michelle was encouraged by her manager to succeed him as manager of technical services within the company's largest division. This promotion was considered by most to be a role that would require significant stretch on Michelle's part, particularly in her ability to lead older and more experienced team members. While some were dubious, Kelvin stood behind the promotion and stated he would continue to mentor Michelle in the leadership space. When Michelle inquired whether her experience matched the competencies required for the role, she was told that her strongest attribute was her 'potential'. She had heard this several times before, yet struggled to put meaning around how the word applied to her. All Michelle knew for sure was that 'potential' implied great expectations.

Over the next three years, Michelle immersed herself in the role, met some huge expectations through long hours — often at the expense of a social life — and continued to learn more about the company by volunteering her time on some innovative projects. Kelvin was still adamant that she not allow herself to be pigeon-holed as one-dimensional. This strategy appeared to pay off when Michelle was asked to take the role of Group Deputy Chief Operating Officer (COO), a position usually considered an early stepping stone to the executive table. *Go for it*, Kelvin and others coached her. *You're making history here. You've just turned thirty and you're a heartbeat away from an executive office! No one this young has ever done that here before.* For Michelle, these thoughts weren't exhilarating. Instead, she was feeling more anxious and under pressure, although she couldn't quite put her finger on why. And yet she walked into the COO's office two days later and accepted the role.

> **Over the next three years, Michelle immersed herself in the role and met some huge expectations through long hours — often at the expense of a social life.**

As Group Deputy COO, Michelle had broad exposure to the executive team around critical discussions and decisions that required her to present and take a view. Once again, she immersed herself in the role, working with an external business coach who had been COO at Disney in Orlando. However, many of the ideas that Michelle brought to the executive table had been incubated in discussions with her business coach, even though she presented them as her own. In reality, Michelle had begun to rely more and more on the external business coach to drill down deep around the technicalities, while she focused primarily on stakeholder management. In the eyes of the executive team, Michelle was delivering on both fronts, and the Group COO loved that she was living up to those big expectations. Just one year after Michelle won the deputy role, the Group COO nominated her for an industry achievement award, and to everyone's delight she won, once again acknowledged at the ceremony for trailblazing — as the youngest recipient in the award's 25-year history.

THE SITUATION

Nova's strategic intent was to always expand globally, and to do so aggressively in both the European and the Asia Pacific markets. Sydney would be the base for the Asia Pacific region, and the analysts were stoked by early signs from some major potential investors, including a Chinese government subsidiary with deep pockets. Nova's CEO summoned his executive team to California for a two-day meeting to focus on global expansion, with the second day dedicated solely to naming Asia Pacific's leadership team. The Asia Pacific CEO was already in place and attended the meeting as well. The critical role that took up most of the time and generated a very heated discussion was the Asia Pacific COO role, which required someone with an extensive background in systems integration and leading large-scale change.

The debate vacillated between various selection criteria, including nationality, global experience, business acumen, and stakeholder management — particularly managing lobbyists and political obstacles across multiple countries. Michelle's name was tabled early on by Kelvin and two others, who were clearly in a strong alliance. A field of four candidates narrowed to two, Michelle being one of them. The other was Ed Manley, who had joined Nova in its first year, hired as a technical analyst by Kelvin, and had gone on to serve in four other big roles. Because Michelle and Ed were peers and both reported to the COO, this meant that the COO's voice would be prominent and persuasive at this meeting, as he had the most direct knowledge of both candidates' capabilities.

In the end, the COO, backed by Kelvin and his alliance, decided that Michelle represented the future and that she exemplified the very potential (that word again) that underpinned their growth strategy. Yes, they acknowledged that Ed was probably more capable on each of the competencies when viewed in isolation; he had deeper experience than Michelle. But they made the case that Michelle was more well-rounded, more intuitive in her read on people and opportunities, and quicker on a learning curve. They also considered her an ideal diversity candidate in relation to the company's talent strategy. After nearly an hour of debate and discussion, the executive team made the call to back Michelle Stanson for the role. Kelvin and the COO were asked to meet with Michelle that evening at an impromptu dinner to persuade her to seize this opportunity.

Several miles high over the Pacific, as Michelle settled into her seat on the Qantas flight, she reflected on her decision to take the role and move to Sydney. Kelvin had put tremendous pressure on her following that fateful dinner when she was overwhelmed to learn that the executive team backed her for such a critical role. She had never considered that she would be the subject of an intensive debate around the executive table. She learned from Kelvin that the global marketing director and the chief legal counsel were both huge advocates. What had she done to win their strong favour? And what about the selection criteria? Neither Kelvin nor the COO went into specific detail, but she knew that Ed had more pertinent experience. She liked Ed. He had been her manager in the first rotation of her accelerated development programme, just 10 short years ago. *Had she surpassed Ed in terms of raw capability? What did they see in her that they hadn't seen in Ed?* 'You've got the potential to take us to great heights, Michelle.' Those words rolled around in her brain over and over, as she succumbed to the inevitable nap that always overtook her 15 minutes into any flight. *'You're going to take us to great heights, Michelle.'* As her head tilted toward one side, Michelle's brow was furrowed in a tight knot. Even as she slept, the fear of disappointing so many people was her foremost concern.

WHAT SYMPTOMS OF IMPOSTOR SYNDROME DO YOU SEE IN MICHELLE?

In her early thirties, Michelle is the prototype of a 'high-potential' and fast-tracking young manager who finds herself on a trajectory toward senior roles in the company. Like most high potentials who are identified early in a talent management process, she knows there are expectations on her to perform to a higher standard than others and to deliver superb work. After joining Nova and being selected to participate in the accelerated development programme, Michelle considered herself to be in a fishbowl, with a number of people keenly observing how she was progressing across the various assignments. Michelle had no firm grasp on what people meant by 'high potential', but it seemed to imply that she was expected to do better than most. This was confirmed in her first rotation assignment in IS, when her manager told her that Nova had high expectations and she would be appraised accordingly, particularly since it was presumed she would one day become a general manager.

Even though Michelle loved the hands-on assignment in IS, she started to deduce that technical experts were not as valued or appreciated as those who were tracking toward management roles. Unfortunately, many companies send this message to their younger talent, downplaying their potential contribution as technical experts and moving them quickly into stretch roles toward management, sometimes beyond their interests or capability. As is the case with Michelle, this often proves to be rich and fertile soil for Impostor Syndrome.

While appreciating her quick advancement at Nova, Michelle found herself to be on-edge and under pressure most of the time. On weekends and even when on holiday, Michelle wasn't able to switch off, as she was always focused on the next challenge and the next performance appraisal. Getting anything less than the highest grade on a performance appraisal was unacceptable. On her second rotation in the accelerated programme, she obsessed for nearly a week after receiving an appraisal that she considered 'average'. Michelle gained a reputation in Nova for being a tough grader of herself. Indeed, some of her managers found it difficult to give her constructive feedback out of concern that she would internalise it in a bad way.

As part of the accelerated programme, Michelle was required to complete a performance feedback survey at the end of her first year. She minimised the positive feedback and focused nearly all her attention on others' perceptions that she seemed inflexible, rigid and defensive. This was a shock for Michelle, and her inner Critic prodded her to do better, which only enhanced the pressure to perform to an even higher standard. She didn't want to disappoint those who believed in her. What Michelle didn't appreciate then was that she was in a vicious cycle that would only increase in intensity over time and with future promotions.

What Michelle didn't appreciate then was that she was in a vicious cycle that would only increase in intensity over time and with future promotions.

Like many who experience Impostor Syndrome, Michelle is largely driven and energised by external validation rather than her own internal sense of satisfaction. She invests a lot of effort into projecting an image of perfection, which only entraps her more deeply across time. What's more, with each promotion toward general management roles, Michelle has become less clear about the tangible metrics of success that were more obvious earlier in her career. Even with her most recent promotion, Michelle is uncertain why she has been selected over Ed, someone she considers more qualified for the role. More than likely the team in Sydney will meet an anxious, guarded and 'all about business' new COO whose major goal in that first month will be to prove to them that she is worthy of the role, even if she is yet to convince herself of the same.

DANIEL LI
NEW HR DIRECTOR, EXTERNAL APPOINTMENT

THE BACKGROUND

At seven in the morning, Daniel Li settled into his chair at the desk which enabled him to look out at the dark sky, still awaiting the first glimpses of a very young day. Daniel stared out into the darkness and rubbed his eyes, suddenly fighting a wave of fatigue that seemed to engulf him. Only in recent days had he begun to think more and more about the nature and pace of his 'average day' since starting with Canexo, a major telecommunications company specialising in underground cable technology.

Daniel had been with Canexo for less than four weeks, but he was already gaining a reputation for keeping long hours. Given his role as newly appointed HR director, Daniel was particularly sensitive to others' perceptions that he was a workaholic. Worse than that, he winced when a peer had told him a week earlier that some of the staff had been debating about whether to invite him out to social events, fearing that he was not making much traction on building a social life in his new town. *A workaholic with no social life,* Daniel thought. *I'm really making a good impression around here.* It occurred to him that few people at work even knew that he was engaged to his long-term girlfriend, Amy, who would soon be moving from Wellington to join him.

Daniel clicked on his screen-saver and discovered that he had neglected to close the email he had been reading the previous evening before he left the office. The email was the announcement of his appointment as HR manager for the Consumer Insights division, sent out to all Canexo staff nearly three months ago, just days after he had submitted his resignation to the law firm that had employed him for nine years. Upon joining Canexo, Daniel had not deleted the announcement, and on occasion he found himself opening it to read about himself. Just as he had done the night before, Daniel scrolled through the email on the screen:

> After an extensive search, we are pleased to announce that Daniel Li, previously with Bettle & Kearns law firm, will be joining the Consumer Insights division as HR director and a member of the CI Executive Team. Daniel has an impressive and varied background as a solicitor in employment law and he will bring a wealth of experience to CI, including his direct role in building and strengthening important customer relationships. The selection committee was most impressed with Daniel's history and talent for driving culture change, a major priority over the next few years for the CI Executive Team. Daniel will be relocating from Wellington to Head Office within the next two months to join our team. We look forward to welcoming Daniel and reaping the benefits of his wisdom and experience.
>
> Terry McNagle, CEO
> Consumer Insights Division

As Daniel read the email for what might easily be the fiftieth time, his mind kept focusing on the words 'history and talent for driving culture change', thinking back to the interview and how convincingly he had talked about his role on several big client projects at B&K. *Had he over-emphasised his leadership role on those projects? Had he gone too far in claiming to have 'deep experience' with a framework he had learned about just months before at an HR conference? And had he been that skilful at sidestepping or surfing specific questions about the role he could play in helping to lead the CI executive team through a major culture initiative called QUEST?* These questions rolled around in Daniel's mind as the sun began to rise, well before any of his staff or peers would arrive to start their day.

This wasn't Daniel's first experience with self-doubt, particularly in the face of carving out new territory to define as his own, which was why this sudden surge was top of mind for him. He had been here before, and was surprised that he was not facing these current doubts with more resilience. Daniel had always seemed to defy the logical path to anything, dropping out of high school from boredom and then studying for two years to qualify for university while working full-time. His path to becoming an employment lawyer certainly wasn't a traditional one either. Daniel had taken a large concentration of history and arts courses while at university in preparation for a career that would stimulate his thinking daily. That had been his mantra earlier in life. As a second-year student, he took a sociology course taught by a gifted attorney who had represented the common man in pursuit of justice against large corporates. Daniel found this whole realm exciting and important, and he grew increasingly interested in employment law, eager to jump in, explore the territory and determine where he could do important work.

After two years with Bettle & Kearns, Daniel gained a reputation for routinely going 'off the beaten track' to get a successful outcome. He had a gift for sourcing and networking resources across and beyond the firm, making things happen quickly around him. Daniel was also masterful with managing account relationships, which were typically reserved for board partners, and the board's confidence in Daniel grew steadily year after year. It was no surprise that Daniel was tracking toward partner status, but he would have to wait at least another five years for serious consideration, and his interests had begun to shift a bit. He joined the regional HR networking association, initially to prospect for clients, but he soon found himself looking forward to the professional development forums and opportunities to learn about best practice. It was Amy who pointed out to Daniel that he seemed to sound more and more like the HR manager than the rising star in

B&K's employment law practice. This might explain why no one was surprised when Daniel walked in a few months after Amy's observation to announce his decision to leave B&K to join Canexo. Everything seemed right about what he was going to do, once again off the beaten track.

THE SITUATION

An incoming email grabbed Daniel's attention. Today was an important day, as he was scheduled to present a high-level overview of the implementation strategy for QUEST to get input from his peers on the CI executive team. It would be his first opportunity to showcase his thinking about the state of the business and the advantages that QUEST presented to drive innovation as a core value. Daniel had spent the past two weeks buried in Google searches on best practice in building innovative cultures, pulling through some key insights. As he went through the final edits on his PowerPoint presentation, Daniel couldn't help but think that very little of what he would present later in the day reflected his own personal experience. He didn't think of himself as an expert on culture change. *How had he managed to put so much emphasis on himself as a change agent in the interview?* Daniel had spent hours exploring the various options for how to best implement QUEST. When he had met with his peers on the CI executive team about their expectations, it became clear that they wanted Daniel to build a coalition of support for the project throughout the division. And that would turn out to be Daniel's biggest worry: he had never led a change project of the scope and scale of QUEST before.

Daniel hadn't anticipated that members of the CI HR team, who now reported to him, would pose the biggest challenge to the strategy he would present later that day. But that was indeed the case, and Daniel knew what was causing a big part of the rift. While he had known there were internal candidates for the HR director role when he applied, Daniel didn't know anything about them and just assumed that he was better qualified, thereby justifying his selection. After joining the team, Daniel learned more about the two people who had been turned down for the role, both of whom had been with Canexo for over 10 years. Between them, they had 28 years of solid HR experience, one of them having spent four years earlier in his career with Canexo's major competitor. In contrast, Daniel hadn't followed the traditional HR path. He considered his background more eclectic, and most of his thinking about HR frameworks and models had evolved through informal study and from his work with an executive coach back at B&K. And while the search committee had been impressed that Daniel was pursuing a graduate certification in HR management studies, all of that seemed minuscule now as he thought about how members of his own team would certainly be questioning his competence to serve as HR director for the CI division. And why shouldn't they? After all, wasn't he starting to have those same doubts?

As Daniel tinkered with the words on one of the slides, he flashed back to memories of the previous week's meeting with the HR leadership team. That had been his second attempt to get the team's buy-in to support the major principles that would serve as the foundation for QUEST. Daniel had been advocating for a flatter structure, which he believed would enable an easier flow of creative thinking and quicker decision-making across the division. However, it had become clear to Daniel that three key players at his leadership table, including the two who had not been selected for the director's role, were not in agreement with him.

Before he could sell the plan to the executive team, Daniel would have to work harder to convince his own team that they should get behind the strategy he was now driving. He had spent the past two weeks in a quandary about the best way to do that. Trying to be supportive, Amy had suggested he use a more engaging approach with his HR team to get their buy-in, but Daniel didn't take well to that idea. While rationally he knew it was the right thing to do, his intuition nagged him into believing that his HR team would only have further doubts about his ability to lead if he went down that path. Daniel didn't want to self-inflict more worries than he already had.

Daniel had even raised the dilemma with Terry McNagle at their weekly catch-up the previous week, but he quickly sensed that the division CEO was a bit irritated by how tentative he seemed. *That's why we selected you over those other two,*' Terry had stated emphatically. *'I didn't want the same old solutions to the same old* problems. *We knew you would come in and shake up the thinking at the HR table. That's why I hired you, Daniel. If you need to make some changes at your own table, then go for it! But let's not waste time here. I'm counting on you to help make QUEST a company-wide initiative beyond Consumer Insights.'* It was only after that conversation that Daniel realised how much Terry was banking on QUEST — and him — to help shine a favourable spotlight on the entire division.

As more people arrived to start their day, Daniel suddenly became aware of how long he had been staring at the laptop screen, deep in thought. Here he was preparing for the most important presentation of his career, and not only was he having major doubts about his own credibility to lead QUEST, but he was also beginning to think he had made a huge mistake by leaving B&K to join Canexo. But it was too late now. He would have to snap out of it and go in there today with a steely determination to look and sound confident. After all, he had been brought on board to be a change agent — to help turn things around. He picked up one of his newly printed business cards from the gold-framed holder that Amy had given him a few years back. The card read: *Daniel Li, HR Director, Consumer Insights Division, Canexo.* *'Yeah, right,'* Daniel muttered to himself as he turned his focus back to the screen. He had to get his head in the game and do it now.

WHAT SYMPTOMS OF IMPOSTOR SYNDROME DO YOU SEE IN DANIEL?

Daniel has a history of bucking the trend and taking the untraditional path toward new opportunities. But he had never before taken such a huge leap of faith when he decided to leave a company in which he had built a very credible and impressive reputation. If he was good enough to be considered a potential partner at B&K, Daniel sensed he could take on the challenges associated with running human resources at Canexo. He trusted his instinct to go for the role, but he hadn't anticipated the challenges he would face in wearing two leadership hats — one as director of the HR team for the CI division, the other as a member of the CI division executive team. One new hat was going to be challenging enough, but two at the same time? While Daniel had no doubt that his reputation at B&K had helped bolster his credibility with the search committee at Canexo, he was having some serious doubts about the leadership challenges he now faced, particularly with his HR team.

Like Daniel, many external appointments who are hired because they 'bring something different to the table' or 'will shake things up' often feel a certain pressure to prove themselves immediately, sensing that others may be sizing them up or, in the worst-case scenario, plotting their demise. The pressure is almost always exacerbated when there are internal candidates who did not get the role and have to report to the new hire who did. To add a final straw, the announcement from Terry had cited Daniel's 'extensive experience' as one of the major reasons he was selected for the role. Daniel assumed that this announcement had gone down like a lead balloon with the two internal candidates who would have known that he had never run an HR team before.

Once on board, Daniel hadn't experienced any overt hostility or tension between himself and the two internal candidates. In fact, one of them had gone out of his way to welcome Daniel on board. Yet he couldn't help feeling that these guys were monitoring his every move and decision, making judgements about his competence and trying to decide whether they would get behind him. When it became clear that neither of these guys agreed with his approach to implement QUEST, Daniel took this as confirmation that they doubted his competence. Rather than trying to involve these two guys in building the implementation plan together, Daniel chose instead to keep them at a distance, unwilling to let them anywhere close to his own doubts and insecurities. And while this all seemed counter-intuitive to what he might otherwise do, Daniel's overwhelming fear of failing to deliver on QUEST and letting Terry down, so very early in his tenure, began to occupy most of his head space.

Like many who experience Impostor Syndrome, Daniel has imposed unrealistic expectations on himself, driven by his manager and others who hope that he will justify their decision to go with an external appointment. And because those who consider themselves to be impostors are inclined to 'suffer in silence', Daniel is left to ponder some important choices without any objective input from someone who might test or challenge his assumptions. He is especially reluctant to solicit ideas from his team or his manager. In four short weeks, Daniel's sole intent is to live up to the pedigree of the person in the hiring announcement. Consequently, people have learned very little about him and have come to experience him as guarded and closed, overly serious, not particularly engaging, and unwilling or unable to show any vulnerability. Ironically, in an attempt to put his best foot forward, the new HR manager is quickly sinking in a quagmire of his own making!

PETER REILLY
SENT TO BRAZIL TO FIX A HUGE MESS

THE BACKGROUND

While Peter Reilly didn't know exactly why he had been summoned to the chief executive's office with little notice, in a call from the CEO's assistant just after noon, he did have some idea of the topic. 'Bob would like to see you today at five if that's convenient for you,' the assistant had said. 'I'll be there,' said Peter, all the while wondering if anyone ever dared to say 'No, that's not convenient for me.' He chose not to test the waters on this occasion, and had spent the next three hours trying to reach his manager, Seth. Little did Peter know at the time that Seth had submitted his resignation just an hour prior to the assistant's call asking him to meet with Bob. It seemed there was a lot of frenetic energy in motion that day on the executive floor at Regis Foods.

Thousands of miles away in São Paulo, Regis Foods' Brazilian joint venture partner, Cantora Holdings, was fighting off bad publicity and growing scrutiny about poor quality-testing through its entire supply chain, including wheat and wheat by-products supplied by Regis. The story was taking on scandalous proportions in Brazil, prompting a week of emergency meetings with senior executives within Regis, including Seth, who had been largely absent and unavailable over the past week. So Peter wasn't surprised when Seth hadn't answered his phone, and he didn't bother calling again, feeling that he had covered himself by leaving a message to advise Seth of the meeting with Bob. Regis had a defined chain-of-command protocol. Under normal circumstances, you would never jump the chain without approval from your 'one-up' manager. But Peter had the feeling that today didn't qualify as normal circumstances. And in 45 minutes, he would find out exactly how right he was.

Peter was widely known and respected, nationally and globally, and he was affectionately regarded as the 'go-to man' for any issues that required high-level diplomacy and negotiation.

Peter had grown up in the agri-business sector, from his early days as a young strategy analyst fresh out of university, to his lobbyist and liaison roles with regional and central government stakeholders — including frequent encounters with the prime minister — to more recent roles in supply chain and logistics that tested his mettle for wearing a general manager hat. Peter was widely known and respected, nationally and globally, and he was affectionately regarded as the 'go-to man' for any issues that required high-level diplomacy and negotiation. Regis had done a good job of recognising and promoting him over the years, signifying how important he was to the business. Peter was especially appreciative of how thoughtful and considerate the Regis family had been during his wife Raewyn's bout with breast cancer three years back. Following a double mastectomy, Raewyn had rebounded with much vigour and strength, and life had stabilised once more for the Reilly family.

The meeting with Bob was a lot shorter than Peter had imagined. He had been correct in assuming that the urgency behind the meeting request had something to do with the crisis in Brazil. But he had no idea, until learning that Seth had resigned, that his stakes in the whole scenario would rise significantly in just the span of a few days. Bob told him that Regis was trying hard to avoid the turmoil and scrutiny of a Brazilian investigation into allegations of intentional tampering with semolina, one of several wheat by-products, to open up greater volume in the global supply chain. Peter knew Bob to be a CEO of strong moral character, and this crisis in Brazil was bringing Bob's values to light. Peter could tell that Bob was deeply troubled by the allegations and the potential blemish on Regis's global reputation. What Bob didn't know at the time was that an investigation would eventually find that the tampering had occurred with a local Brazilian supplier, not Regis. Untainted by the knowledge of that eventual outcome, Peter was both humbled and honoured that afternoon when the CEO asked him to go to Brazil to manage the crisis and stabilise the business.

THE SITUATION

Two days on the ground in Brazil, nearly a full week after the meeting with Bob, Peter held his first meeting with the Regis Brazil leadership team. Things had certainly moved swiftly across the week. First there had been Seth's resignation, followed two days later by the announcement that the president of Regis Brazil would be stepping down within two weeks, and that Peter would be stepping in as interim president to run the business. The week had truly been a blur, with Peter receiving dozens of congratulatory and 'atta-boy' emails from friends and colleagues, both internal and external, moving frantically between meetings, and trying his best to check in with Raewyn whenever he could to see how she was coping with the sudden change of events. The evening before he had left for Brazil on this trip, he and Raewyn had spent a couple of hours over dinner talking through the logistics of how to make it all happen. Peter had never really consulted with Raewyn over the decision. In fact, he hadn't really consulted with himself either, having been put on the spot by Bob, who frankly wasn't asking but was telling him he was going to Brazil to lead the company out of this crisis. This was 'emergency succession-planning' in its purest form.

Peter managed through the first meeting with the Brazilian team, exercising extreme caution and tiptoeing softly around the issue of the change in leadership. He had met the day before with the sitting president, who had confided in him that the situation had worsened two weeks earlier when it was clear that the Minister of Commerce had lost confidence in him, prompting the decision to have him step down. And it made sense that Regis would opt to bring in Peter, an experienced and skilled arbitrator who could help repair and rebuild these very important relationships. The rationale and logic made sense to Peter on this front. Crisis management — he had done that before. Negotiating and building relationships with top government officials — this was also familiar territory for him. *But run the business?* This was definitely a new space for Peter, even if it was only on an interim basis. It hadn't made sense to him when Bob had first talked with him about it a week earlier. It hadn't made sense to him when he had played it back to Raewyn that same evening. And it still wasn't making sense to him, just hours after his first meeting with his new team. Peter had never run a commercial P&L (profit-and-loss business) in his entire career. And here he was, sitting in São Paulo, the newly appointed interim president of Regis's largest market in South America. Suprisingly, Peter found it all quite intimidating.

For the next week Peter was immersed in meetings with members of his new team and with the outgoing president, as well as quick telephone calls and a couple of 'meet and greet' coffees and lunches with government officials and other key stakeholders. He was learning his way around the macro edges of the business, finding himself more comfortable after each conversation, but being very careful not to dive too deeply into the performance of the business. Peter kept one of the younger staff members, Andre, at his side most hours of the work day, finding him to be a wealth of knowledge and information. Somehow he didn't mind letting Andre educate him about the business and help him navigate his way around. Andre reminded him of himself years earlier, a bright and eager analyst who was very smart about most things, with a real eagerness to help the new boss. Peter didn't feel that same level of comfort with the more experienced and senior members of his new team. He had sensed at the first and subsequent meetings that he would have to keep his guard up more with them, careful not to fuel any concerns that the new president, even if interim, knew very little about running a business.

With Seth gone, Peter was now reporting to Brad Singletary, the executive vice president for Regis Latin America (LATAM). In the meeting with Bob where Peter had learned of his 'promotion', Brad had been conferenced in by phone from Santiago, and it wasn't until a week later that Peter and Brad would sit face-to-face to discuss the challenges at hand. Peter and Brad had known each other for years, and earlier in their careers they had overlapped on a project that was to target international growth markets. How ironic it was that Brazil had been a major focal point of that team's recommendations, as both men were now directly responsible for saving the business from collapse. Brad was due to arrive in São Paulo later in the day, and the two would have dinner together that night. Peter was both eager and anxious to meet with Brad. He needed to get his head around his priorities, and he wanted to learn as much as he could from Brad's in-depth experience. Peter's dilemma was deciding how vulnerable he could be with Brad without causing his new boss to question his confidence and credibility.

What surprised Peter the most about all this was how unsure he seemed to be of his every movement, even the smallest decisions that previously would not have caused him any hesitation whatsoever.

What surprised Peter the most about all this was how unsure he seemed to be of his every movement, even the smallest decisions that previously would not have caused him any hesitation whatsoever. Now he was mulling over everything, second-guessing himself. What had happened to him in the span of a few short weeks? The dinner with Brad would prove to be very illuminating, as Brad would tell him a story about a very similar experience he had faced when he was appointed to his current role two years earlier.

Brad told Peter that the worst few months of his career had been after he was appointed as executive vice president of LATAM. Brad had never worked outside the home country, and, although he had run two smaller domestic product lines within the broader Regis portfolio, nothing could have prepared him for the appointment to run all of Latin America. His appointment had been just as sudden as Peter's, although there was no pressing crisis to exacerbate his insecurities. Nevertheless, Brad had spent far more energy in those first few months hiding his own doubts and fears than he had on letting others around him educate him about the region's businesses. Brad told Peter that he had always considered being on a learning curve to be fun and exciting, but this wasn't the case when he was promoted to run Regis LATAM. Instead of 'fun and exciting', Brad described the first few months as 'intense and draining'.

The breakthrough for Brad had occurred in a similar conversation with Bob, their CEO. Bob had told Brad that he hadn't been promoted to the LATAM role for his regional knowledge, but rather for his experience as a general manager — for his ability to manage a broader system, to manage relationships, and to prioritise the region's goals against Regis's global strategy. Bob hadn't expected Brad to be an expert on the Latin region's businesses or markets. He already had experts on his team who could advise him on those matters. Bob had told Brad, as Brad was now telling Peter, that he was promoted because of his management acumen — for his ability to think, build relationships, drive his team toward better decisions, and tap into the technical and commercial expertise of his staff to make good decisions. As Brad recollected the story for Peter, he laughed out loud after realising that Peter had been experiencing the exact same reaction as he had. And Peter was able to laugh with both relief and sympathy when Brad exclaimed, 'I thought I was the only one who ever went through something like that.' Neither man realised at that dinner that they were talking about Impostor Syndrome. But both could relate to what it feels like to be an impostor, trying hard not to make even the smallest mistake that might expose them as frauds.

WHAT SYMPTOMS OF IMPOSTOR SYNDROME DO YOU SEE IN PETER?

Unlike Michelle and Daniel, both of whom were still climbing their respective career ladders with lots of steps ahead of them, Peter was a seasoned career veteran who had grown up in the agri-business sector and had been with Regis for over two decades. In fact, Peter routinely referred to himself as one of the 'old heads' when talking with younger staff. Impostor Syndrome is no respecter of age or seniority, striking teenagers and their grandparents alike. And even though experienced managers have typically grown more aware of and comfortable with their limitations by middle age, they still experience doubts and insecurities related to how other people appraise them.

> **He hadn't anticipated and was quite surprised when the inner Critic began chattering away vigorously in his ear.**

This is what surprised Peter the most after he learned that Regis was counting on him to help turn things around quickly in Brazil. He hadn't anticipated and was quite surprised when the inner Critic began chattering away vigorously in his ear.

Even though Peter was literate about Regis's business portfolio, he had never been held to account for the bottom-line performance of a major P&L. In fact, the largest budget Peter had managed sat across a large swathe of their supply chain, just under $9.5 million. The Brazilian business alone accounted for 22 per cent of the LATAM portfolio, somewhere in the vicinity of $52 million. In that initial week following his new assignment, Peter had immersed himself in the numbers, struggling to make sense of some of the basics. Fortunately, one of his closest friends was the commercial director for a global transport company. Before leaving for Brazil, Peter spent four hours with her asking dozens of questions and trying to establish some priorities for his meeting with the Brazilian CFO, who would now be reporting to him and expecting some guidance from his new boss. Even after spending hours with his friend, Peter felt woefully unprepared. And there was very little he could do about it in the short term.

It was only after his dinner with Brad that Peter realised he had been way too harsh on himself by downplaying all the experience he was bringing to the role. What Regis needed more than anything else right now in Brazil was an experienced and well-rounded executive, one who was both comfortable and skilled in mending and building relationships, particularly at top government levels. And although these attributes defined Peter's peak skills as an executive, he had somehow downplayed the significance of this profile and his impressive track record, choosing instead to focus on the fact that he had never run a business before. The extra pressure of the business being in major crisis certainly added fire to the inner Critic's voice, reminding Peter that he couldn't make a single misstep in this new role. Whereas Peter was playing this challenge through a commercial lens, Regis was counting on him to play it through the lens of a senior statesman.

What Brad did for Peter was to normalise a phenomenon that Peter assumed was personal and something that only he was aware of. When you think you are going through something that no one else can understand or relate to, there is a tendency to suffer in silence. It is not until someone else, particularly someone with Brad's credibility, opens up and replicates what you have been thinking and feeling that it begins to seem less menacing. Senior leaders can help normalise Impostor Syndrome by telling stories about their own personal quest to discover authentic leadership for themselves. To hear a CEO or a senior executive recall what it was like to work through periods of vulnerability and self-doubt can go a long way to helping younger managers come to terms with a phenomenon that is not just 'in their own heads'.

A.J., MICHELLE, DANIEL AND PETER:
WHAT THEY ALL HAVE IN COMMON

A.J., Michelle, Daniel and Peter are four very different people with different backgrounds and life experiences. What they all have in common is the vulnerability each has experienced when placed in a situation requiring them to stretch their capability into a new space. For A.J., the vulnerability was associated with sizing herself up in relation to a room full of strangers. In the case of Michelle and Peter, the company asked them to step up to a specific challenge. For Daniel, he made that choice himself. Yet the similarity in their reactions goes to the heart of a phenomenon that made each of them feel like an impostor in their roles.

Like our four characters, people who are successful tend to perpetuate high expectations from others and themselves. It is not necessarily what has been explicitly stated so much as what is inferred, and this is the main reason people find it hard to talk about. It is like privately raising your own personal bar on what defines success, sometimes even higher than others around you would find reasonable. Not only is it untenable for you to reach these unreasonable standards, but you are reluctant or unable to talk about it when you can't. So at the very point where you might benefit the most from some objective input from your manager or a peer, you are probably the most closed or guarded, worried that you will reinforce their worst fears about your capability.

As people grow their careers in companies, stretch is often associated with moving away from technical expertise and moving more toward the space of management. When we talk about 'growing capability' in employees, we are typically focused on the roles we see them moving toward, which means we have to stretch them to test and build new skills. The vulnerability kicks in when you ask people to move away from something they love doing (because that is what they are really good at) and ask them to take on bigger responsibility in an area where they are less certain and have little or no experience.

The space of 'management' is not a good space for many people who perceive that it is the only path to advancement, even if it means moving into murkier waters to get there. Those accused of being 'micro-managers' can perhaps relate to this phenomenon — they gravitate toward and are energised by the technical space much more so than the management space. Against their best intentions, micro-managers sometimes can't help diving back into the more comfortable space of 'doing', as it validates their sense of self-worth and of feeling valued.

Companies that encourage stretch to test and grow their younger talent need to be mindful that these future leaders require both self-awareness and skills to help navigate those murky waters of transition. Too often, some of our most promising 'rising stars' are left to figure it out for themselves.

There's an intriguing paradox about Impostor Syndrome — as common as it is, very few people assume others can relate to it or understand it.

11.

Frames: Getting at the root cause of Impostor Syndrome

WHAT ARE FRAMES?

A frame is a mental construct you put around something in order to give it meaning. You start developing frames from the moment you are born. In fact, social anthropologists suggest that you are born with an inclination toward certain frames, the instinctive bond between a mother and newborn being one example. By the time you are two years old, you have developed hundreds of frames for the experience commonly known as 'life'. And, just like a fingerprint, the multitude of frames that help you navigate your way through life are unique to you. No two people on Earth have identical frames — that is why people who witness the same event walk away with different interpretations of what happened. Even though we often want to paint things as 'black or white', the reality of multiple frames reminds us that most of life falls into that wide realm of 'grey'.

You automatically and subconsciously put frames around everything. And these frames, which reside largely in the background

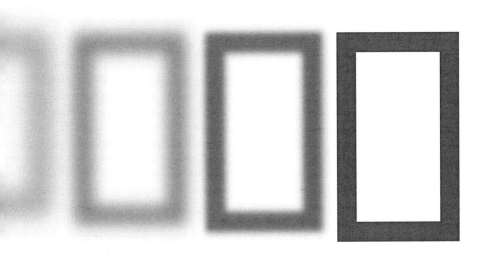

of your thinking, help you make it through the day. You have a frame for how you start your day, choosing to shower and dress before you eat breakfast, or even choosing whether to have breakfast. You have a frame for how best to commute to work, or even whether work is commutable. You have a frame for who you are, in relation to others, at work. You have a frame for your boss. You have a frame for being a boss. You have a frame for what you consider to be a good teammate, and chances are you relate to that person differently than you do to another person who doesn't match that frame. You have a frame for what success looks like on a very important project. When your frame for success differs from your teammate's frame, the tension is often referred to as a 'creative difference'. And on either side of a creative difference, you typically have two or more people who have placed each other in frames. Frames are all around you, and they help define your experience with life. And they also help define your experience with yourself.

HOW FRAMES FORM

It makes sense that frames are formed largely from personal experience; you tend to frame something as favourable if it brings a positive outcome, and unfavourable if the end result is negative. For example, many people frame 'feedback' as a negative construct, as it has become associated with painful critiquing or personal consequences. So when you hear people say that 'feedback is a gift', it may run counter to your experience of feedback. Another example highlights a positive frame around what you consider a 'trusted colleague' to be. Someone who is not driven by a sense of personal gain, but is instead motivated by what is best for the business, may fit this frame for you.

> **You have many frames in your head that help or hinder how you assess people in terms of their capability. A good number of your frames probably fall into the category of 'conventional wisdom', operating just below the level of conscious decision and choice.**

Beyond direct personal experience, you are also inclined to put a frame around something based on 'conventional wisdom'. These are widely held beliefs that are often untested and, in many cases, unfounded. For example, the frame that women are not suitable for military combat was prevalent for centuries under the common paradigm of warfare. There weren't substantive or tangible data to support this frame, yet it stood as a barrier for women who chose military service as a profession, one only recently being lifted in the United States, for example, after decades of challenge to the discriminatory policy.

You have many frames in your head that help or hinder how you assess people in terms of their capability. A good number of your frames probably fall into the category of 'conventional wisdom', operating just below the level of conscious decision and choice. The US basketball player Jason Collins, who announced in 2013 that he is gay, reminded us that frames rooted in common wisdom can often limit our realm of what is possible. After Collins's announcement, it almost seemed ridiculous to believe that 'being gay' and 'playing professional basketball' were incompatible frames. But that is how conventional wisdom works: it is conventional until and unless you find data that suggest otherwise.

You also form frames based on who, or what, you deem credible, even if it defies conventional wisdom or logic. Young kids adopt a lot of their parents' and older siblings' frames, largely a function of the credence we put on the words of those who are authority figures in our lives. As you grew up and matured, you were likely to be influenced by the frames of the teachers, mentors and coaches you respected. It is no different at work and in your professional life. A lot of the frames that govern how you conduct yourself professionally have been shaped by previous managers whom you have respected and, in some cases, chosen to emulate. You are very likely to pay close attention to your manager's frames, often adjusting your own accordingly. That is how it works in situations where you are trying to fit in and have others frame you as 'acceptable'.

A company's culture reflects a number of complementary and overlapping frames. When you choose to join a company, you often don't know much about the deep-rooted frames that underlie how people operate and how business gets done. But as you immerse yourself in the company culture, there is a slow and subtle process that unfolds whereby you work hard to reconcile any differences between your personal frames and what you are learning about the company's frames. There is a psychological term called *cognitive dissonance*, which basically suggests that you don't like to think of yourself as a hypocrite. You typically resolve the dissonance in one of two ways, either by modifying the way you think or act to adjust to the new frame, or by choosing not to change your frame and exiting the situation.

Studies on dissonance suggest that you are more likely to modify your personal frames in order to fit in, especially if you hold the company, or your manager, in high regard. Consider the last time your manager coached you to put a different frame around a situation, or even around yourself. The degree to which you modified your frame would have been directly related to how much credence you put in that manager's expertise and authority. If you are still there, chances are you modified your frame. The reality is: people adopt or modify a good number of their frames in order to fit with the norm. This is another way of saying that fitting in is a prevalent frame that most of us carry around in our heads. You have been making these choices throughout your life. If you can't make a personal frame fit in with a company, or your manager, or in a relationship, you typically leave — but you often try really hard to make things work before you make that choice.

HOW FRAMES WORK

Frames mostly help you navigate through life. As you grow, you develop mental structures for everything you encounter. It is a plausible theory that the more experienced you are with life, the more resilient you are with whatever life has to throw your way. People who face crises of confidence and resilience are often facing a particular adverse scenario for the first time. It could be the first time you have grieved the loss of a good friend, your first experience of being made redundant, or even of something positive like being promoted into a bigger role. If you don't already have a frame for a sudden change — whether positive or negative — it can throw you. This could well explain why, in the absence of a proper induction, over half of senior executives de-rail within 18 months of being promoted to a bigger role. As with direct experience, induction helps to build frames for dealing with the expected and the unexpected.

Frames give you something to hold on to in the face of uncertainty. They help you feel less anxious in situations where you are not in total control of the outcome.

Frames give you something to hold on to in the face of uncertainty. They help you feel less anxious in situations where you are not in total control of the outcome. In a business context, you will see frames play out in ways that reflect cross-cultural differences. In Japan, rigorous debate with passionate advocacy on both sides is frowned upon as discourteous and disrespectful. That is not the case in some Latin cultures, where passion (and even anger) is viewed as a key attribute of integrity. These are two different frames which you would likely call upon should you find yourself doing business in either culture. This is just one of countless examples of how frames will vary across, and even within, cultures.

Frames are funny. They do help you navigate through your day and your life, and they are very useful when you are trying to make your way through ambiguous and uncertain times. But they can also work against you in ways that are sometimes difficult to see. Because your frames typically kick in at the subconscious level — meaning you aren't making a conscious effort to call them up — you have to be very careful that they aren't inhibiting you from seeing and hearing other possibilities; that they are acting as enablers rather than impediments. Carly Fiorina, the former chairman and CEO of Hewlett Packard, tells the story of how, early in her career as a secretary at HP, a mentor encouraged her to broaden her contribution by moving into a bigger role *in* the business. Fiorina's frame for her own development was that she would grow her skills as a secretary. The mentor's frame for her development was broader than her own. Like many of us, Fiorina adjusted her own frame, as influenced by her mentor, and this led her to a new realm of possibilities, culminating in the company's top role.

Another inhibiting feature about frames is how you are inclined to select data to reinforce the frames that are in place. The toughest thing about learning something new is unlearning something old. Once you have a frame for something in place, you look for evidence to lock it in, choosing sometimes to overlook perfectly sound evidence that contradicts your way of thinking about yourself, or about another person or situation. For example, if you think of yourself as a weak presenter, you will be inclined to focus on all the things that you didn't do well, rather than on the majority of the presentation which went very well. And if your frame for something is rigidly locked into place, you may not even see the most obvious of contrary data in front of you. That is why there is so much controversy associated with labelling kids in schools, particularly those with learning disabilities. If you begin to think of yourself as disabled, it is only a matter of time before you and others start to lock you into that inhibiting frame. It is no different at work. Once we frame someone as a 'poor performer', it is usually only a matter of weeks before the farewell party.

Just be mindful that your frames, while largely helpful, can also lock you in while locking others out. You don't want your frames to become fortresses that are impenetrable from either side. If your goal is to become more self-aware, you have to get close to your frames to determine which ones are working for you and which ones are impeding your progress. For all of us, there are frames in our heads that are out-dated, irrelevant, irrational — clearly working against personal and professional growth. To become more self-aware, you must first come to terms with the frames that capture the essence of who you are. After all, those are the frames that others see when they are with you, even if you can't.

FRAMING YOURSELF

Image consultants believe that what people see about you on the 'outside' is a direct reflection of what you think about yourself on the 'inside'. If you feel vibrant and think of yourself as a confident person, that is what other people are likely to experience in their interactions with you. If you have entrapped yourself in negative frames that cause you to come across as cynical and distrusting, this will soon work against your ability to influence successful outcomes. In all aspects of your life, what you think and feel about yourself really does matter.

When was the last time you stopped to examine your own personal frames about you? How closely attuned are you to the frames that others have put you in? Is there a relationship between how you see yourself and how others see you? Typically that relationship starts early in life, from the earliest years, even before you could form complete sentences! That's how old some of your personal frames are. They play a big role in defining your self-esteem, and consequently the way others approach and respond to you as a person. If you are dissatisfied with a relationship and want to make it better, a good place to start is usually with yourself.

A positive self-esteem correlates strongly with positive frames about who you are and what you can accomplish. It works the same with negative self-esteem; a sense of pessimism typically travels with unsuccessful outcomes. Since your frames are shaped largely from experience, or the credibility you place on how other people see you, it is important to trace your self-frames to their earliest roots.

Parents, older siblings, peers and those in authority helped to shape most of those early frames. If you heard mostly positive things about your abilities and potential as a young child, it is very likely that your experiences, and the outcomes, were shaped by this 'can do' attitude. If you were led to believe that you are largely incapable and worthless, every negative outcome would only serve to reinforce this frame and a 'no can do' attitude.

These two frames are generally called 'optimism' and 'pessimism', and research suggests that you lean toward one or the other based largely on your experiences of trying to influence outcomes and the results that followed. Positive people have generally been reinforced to think, feel and act positively. Negative people have generally been reinforced to think, feel and act negatively. If you don't like the way you think, feel or behave, chances are you can trace the source back to some early or pivotal experiences that locked you into a particular frame that is now working against you.

To get close to these negative frames that are holding you back, you have to determine whether you can live inside the mega-frame of 'imperfection'.

To get close to these negative frames that are holding you back, you have to determine whether you can live inside the mega-frame of 'imperfection'. You just need to believe that you have more power and control over your destiny than you had previously considered. If your starting point is a frame that says you don't have to be perfect to be loved or appreciated, you are on the right path. However, getting on this path is a lot easier than staying on it. With the acceptance of imperfection comes a greater comfort with vulnerability. And as you will learn later in the book, vulnerability can be a daunting force if you are trying to reframe it in your own head. After all, you have probably spent most of your life trying to minimise its existence. A major reframe of your relationship with vulnerability will serve you well if your goal is to think and feel better about yourself and what you can accomplish. This is something that real impostors are unable to do.

FRAMES OF AN IMPOSTOR

The need to be perfect and to ward off vulnerability fuels the symptoms of Impostor Syndrome. If you have ever been inclined to reach for the impostor's mask, chances are you were trying to distance yourself from negative frames that have worked against you in the past. You are far less likely to get hurt if you entrap yourself in a small but safe zone where you have ultimate control of everything that happens. The problem with this is that you may paralyse yourself in the process! The need to be perfect comes with a heavy price — that price is called 'living'.

Consider the frames below and how deep-rooted they are. You can see how they have a direct bearing on the way other people experience you.

FRAME	IMPOSTOR SYMPTOMS
I'm not very smart	Reluctance to go first or lead with an opinion
I'm not good with numbers	Anxious when speaking about financial matters
I'm plain and uninteresting	Near panic when in a room full of strangers
My peers can't be trusted	Unwilling to disclose important information
Safe is better than sorry	Never stand alone; best to go with the majority view
I don't have what it takes to lead	Quick to volunteer for roles with little visibility
It's not cool to be different here	Overly critical and dismissive of people who stand out or stand alone
You have to be one of the good ol' boys to make it to the top	Uncomfortable wearing anything other than a dark suit with a starched collar and solid tie

You can see the direct relationship between the frames and the symptoms of Impostor Syndrome. When you are in the moment and experiencing the symptoms real-time, it is sometimes hard to make the connection between what you are thinking and how other people may experience you. It is important to remember that most of what you do can be traced to your thinking. If you don't like how others are experiencing you, typically you have to examine and eventually change the way you think.

The proverbial iceberg is another useful metaphor that helps put Impostor Syndrome in perspective. While you are primarily focused on the tip of the iceberg, because that is what you can see, it is the larger mass of the iceberg — what you can't see — that can do the most damage. When you think about stripping away the frames that are the very foundation of Impostor Syndrome, true transformation occurs at the base of the iceberg rather than at the tip. At the tip of the iceberg, you are inclined to find reasons to blame others. Your frames reside at the base of the iceberg, and it is at the base where you can take real ownership for the solution. You can say that you are becoming more self-aware every time you take a peek into one of your existing frames to see if it is working for you or against you.

TRUTHS ABOUT FRAMES

YOUR FRAMES ARE:	
Learned	A product of your direct experience or adopted from someone whom you deem credible
Self-perpetuating	You tend to look for data to support your frames rather than refute them
Interconnected	If you are hard on yourself, you fully expect others to be equally critical of you
Pervasive	From one experience, you are likely to generalise to others
Ossified	Like fossils, your beliefs are deeply imprinted on your psyche
Confronting	You are not really prepared to think of yourself as unkind or unjust
Validating	You are reassured when things turn out the way you predict they will
Informative	Your behaviour patterns tell us a lot about how you think and who you are

These 'truths' about frames make it fairly obvious that your own patterns of thinking can be a formidable force, sometimes working directly against what is in your best interest. To go to the base of the iceberg to change your frames is hard and confronting work. It was the great seventeenth-century philosopher René Descartes who said 'I think, therefore I am.' What you project to the rest of the world is most often a direct reflection of how you think. The deepest work to really overcome Impostor Syndrome resides within you.

FINDING THE ROOT CAUSE
IS HALF THE BATTLE

Going to the base of the iceberg to explore your frames will definitely get you closer to the beliefs and assumptions that others are likely to see through your expressed views and behaviours. But this is easier said than done. Just like anything below the surface of the water, your frames are largely invisible to you. As powerful as they are in influencing how you behave toward others, many of your frames remain a mystery to you. At the tip of the iceberg, you are often very busy, working on multiple priorities at one time, sometimes in a reactive crisis mode. It's no surprise that you find yourself disconnected from your own thinking. You don't always have the time to make the connection between your frames and your behaviour.

There is something curious about how an impostor's frames work. When things go well, an impostor is more likely to attribute the positive outcome to something external. You are likely to hear statements like 'I was lucky' or 'Fate was on my side this time' or 'I was in the right place at the right time'. Notice the tendency to distance any personal effort or skill from the positive outcome. Conversely, if something goes wrong, an impostor is more likely to attribute that negative outcome to a personal liability. In these cases, the impostor will think (but usually not verbalise) statements like 'I wasn't prepared' or 'I never do well with numbers' or 'I'm just not cut out for this role'.

When things go well, an impostor is more likely to attribute the positive outcome to something external . . . Conversely, if something goes wrong, an impostor is more likely to attribute that negative outcome to a personal liability.

An impostor's words are the most tangible clue as to what is going on at the base of the iceberg. But the self-awareness that comes from examining your frames is only half the battle to overcome the syndrome. You have to work hard at another dimension of your being that goes to the heart of your credibility. That dimension is called *authenticity*. Authenticity is the antidote to Impostor Syndrome, and you should think of it as the essence of who you truly are. In the following section, pay close attention to the elements that comprise authenticity. It's time to dig in now around the best way to beat Impostor Syndrome.

12.

Authenticity: Why authentic leadership matters

'Real isn't how you are made,' said the Skin Horse. 'It's a thing that happens to you. When a child loves you for a long, long time, not just to play with, but REALLY loves you, then you become Real.'

'Does it hurt?' asked the Rabbit.

'Sometimes,' said the Skin Horse, for he was always truthful. 'When you are Real you don't mind being hurt.'

'Does it happen all at once, like being wound up,' he asked, 'or bit by bit?'

'It doesn't happen all at once,' said the Skin Horse. 'You become. It takes a long time. That's why it doesn't happen often to people who break easily, or have sharp edges, or who have to be carefully kept. Generally, by the time you are Real, most of your hair has been loved off, and your eyes drop out and you get loose in the joints and very shabby. But these things don't matter at all, because once you are Real you can't be ugly, except to people who don't understand.'

— Margery Williams, *The Velveteen Rabbit*

ABOUT AUTHENTICITY

There is something about authenticity that intrigues people. As with collecting stamps, or coins, or paintings, or vintage cars — we are compelled to them because they are considered to be rare, one of a kind, worth the extra investment to have or to be associated with. Authentic leadership stimulates the same sensation of people wanting some special connection because of who you are and what you represent.

Whether you are a CEO or a team leader or a newly appointed intern, your best weapon of influence is being yourself. The more connections you are able to make with another person, the more likely you will be able to relate to each other and potentially move forward on something you both consider important. It is no different with a team or a group of people. You create bonds through those things you have in common. To find the things you have in common with others, you have to be willing to give of yourself. And to give of yourself simply means you are willing to let others see that you are human. That includes all those things that fall short of perfection.

> **Whether you are a CEO or a team leader or a newly appointed intern, your best weapon of influence is being yourself.**

I have come to admire legendary All Black Sir John Kirwan. Kirwan suffers from chronic depression, and for a good deal of his early adult life and professional career he chose to suffer in silence, afraid that his teammates and fans would consider him weak, or worse, if he chose to make his illness public. But Kirwan decided to come forward and talk openly about depression and the damage it can do to individuals, families and communities. And by doing so he has set an example for many others and paved a way, particularly for boys and men, to acknowledge the devastating impact of an illness that can be treated, and in many cases cured. By making himself human, Kirwan's leadership has brought to light a purpose and a cause that thousands are willing to support him on. It is an example of how getting others to follow your lead is most directly tied to being real about who you are.

If you have made a mistake recently at work, or something didn't turn out the way you had hoped, you are probably more likely to talk about it openly with another colleague or your manager if they are able to relate to what you are going through. You build trust with another person, or with a team, by finding those 'connection points' — those things that you have in common and can relate to. This is why it is important to establish a work environment in which people get a chance to relate to one another as people first, co-workers second. These are 'whole' people who come to work each day, riddled with normality and exuding vapours of imperfection. The way to build trust within a team is to build those connection points and create opportunities for people to support each other, not from a space of obligation, but from a place of genuine empathy.

Your own authenticity — the opportunity to be genuine and real — frees you up to be more focused on others and less focused on you. The less focused you are on what others think about *you*, the more you can be focused on who *they* are and what *they* need. One of my favourite CEO clients, Ken Rivers, was known for telling his employees at Refining NZ the following:

'I'm not perfect, and the one thing you can count on me doing consistently is being wrong about something. Which is where you come in and why you're here. We run this business together, me at the helm and you as the team I can rely on to help get us as close to 'right' as possible. We'll make mistakes along the way, but we're more likely to get it right if we accept that none of us, especially me, is perfect.'

13.

What authentic leadership looks like in business

TRUSTWORTHY

Trust is at the foundation of any strong personal or professional relationship. You are more likely to influence, and be influenced by, another person if there is trust between you. Yet, trust is often depicted as something obtuse or ephemeral that just 'happens' in relationships. Very often, we focus on trust once it has been broken or lost. Leaders who are proactive about their development don't view trust as happenstance, but rather understand the specific elements that can accelerate and build trust.

A person you trust is likely to be credible, consistent, likeable and motivated by something more noble than self-interest. Credibility goes to the person's believability in your eyes. Consistency means that 'who she is' and 'how she is' don't vary across extremes or circumstances. Likeability is driven by quantity and quality. The more time you spend with a person, the more connections you build, which enhances trust. Connections speak to quality: I like you because I can relate to you.

And how you perceive another person's motives goes a long way toward determining if you will open up and render yourself vulnerable.

SWITCHED ON

Authentic people understand the difference between playing political games and showing political savvy in their efforts to influence others. There is a huge difference between the two. People who play political games, or take pride in being 'political', are skilful at relaxing or strengthening their positions on issues, depending on the coalition they are with at the time. The sole objective is to win favour with a particular person or group, adjusting the message accordingly. Little wonder that people often find it difficult to trust politicians.

'Political savvy' is a different beast. It requires you to know your audience and to understand their interests and to appeal for support on the basis of what you have in common, unafraid to take a stand on where you may differ. Being 'switched on' is about appreciating that there is room for a different frame or perspective, even if you can't ultimately support it. People tend to appreciate you more for standing on what you believe rather than telling them what they want to hear for political gain. It is a gift to work with people who are switched on, but aren't political. That's the essence of this attribute.

> **Authentic people understand the difference between playing political games and showing political savvy in their efforts to influence others.**

GENUINELY INTERESTED IN OTHERS

This attribute of authenticity is equally about mindset as it is about skill. Impostors tend to be rigid and inflexible when it comes to looking for value in what others have to contribute. They live in fear that others will devalue their contribution if another idea posed by someone else gets more attention. Therefore, an impostor is likely to look for flaws or holes in other people's ideas, even while feigning interest.

An authentic person is genuinely interested in the thoughts, views and feelings of others, not afraid to focus attention on others, a side benefit being broader involvement and engagement. Authentic people don't lead with the 'need to be right', so you are less likely to experience them as defending a position and more likely to see them using high-quality inquiry to fully understand another view. When you are not worried that another person's view may be more robust than your own, it positions you as someone who can be influenced in a learning conversation. It's not about winning; it's about coming to the best decision.

COURAGE TO BE YOURSELF

In most cases, putting your best foot forward is easier than acknowledging that you have a less-than-perfect foot. Focusing on what you do well is interesting, but not necessarily courageous. The courage to be yourself means you are aware of your shortcomings and liabilities, and your primary objective is not to hide them, but to incorporate them into an integrated perspective on who you are as a person. Are you as comfortable talking about what makes you vulnerable as you are talking about what makes you stellar?

Conversely, some people find it hard to bring focus onto the things they do exceptionally well, choosing instead to hide their strengths below the parapet. As an authentic person, you are at peace with the totality of your persona — the good, the bad and the ugly. Sometimes the real courage comes with believing that others will find you of interest because of, not in spite of, your willingness to show them the whole you. That's what being 'the real deal' is all about. The next

The courage to be yourself means you are aware of your shortcomings and liabilities, and your primary objective is not to hide them, but to incorporate them into an integrated perspective on who you are as a person.

time someone uses that expression to describe you, chances are you have impressed them with your courage to be yourself.

EXHIBITS FLOW AND PASSION

'Being in flow' is a term that signifies your ability to lose yourself in, or become one with, an activity that is both energising and meaningful to you. When in flow, you may seem completely involved or absorbed in a task, not because you have to be, but because you *want* to be. While a particular activity may not necessarily be meaningful or important to everyone, it is clear that a person in flow is engaged with full focus, attention and dedication.

You are able to sense the conviction and real sense of ownership in bringing forward something that reflects pride and personal investment. Examples of people in flow range vastly across the domain of human interests, from total immersion in getting a candidate elected, to losing yourself for hours in writing a song or a poem, to writing a position paper for the board. Think about the last time you used your skills to the utmost for something that was both challenging and important to you. There is an exhilaration that comes with being in flow.

WALKS THE TALK

While 'walking the talk' has become a cliché, it nonetheless still carries a lot of weight, particularly in assessing character. When you perceive hypocrisy in another person, it leaves you wondering about their motive, intent or some hidden agenda. Alignment between words and actions is just as important as consistency of behaviour. You might even argue that they *are* the same, especially since 'what you do' and 'what you say' are both behaviours.

Authentic people can't live in a state of cognitive dissonance. You are likely to experience such dissonance, for example, when you pronounce your belief in healthy nutrition and eating habits, but your daily dietary routine leaves a lot of room for improvement. It is like telling a person that you are going to vote for them, but then doing the exact opposite when you are in the privacy of the voting booth. Senior leaders in organisations have to be especially mindful that perceived hypocrisy between their words and their actions can bring down the very foundation of a values initiative. There are countless examples of how quickly a person can lose credibility and be seen as inauthentic when words and deeds don't match up.

STANDS ON VALUES AND PRINCIPLE

Some things do matter very much to you, and over time people begin to define you by virtue of the stakes you put in the ground and the lines you draw in the sand. If equity is an important value, you remove the barriers to gender equality in compensation schemes. If safety is truly an imperative, you don't try to justify near-misses with excuses or questionable logic. If you believe leadership is about creating an environment for your team to be successful, you are quick to confront bullying as an unacceptable management practice, even at the risk of being bullied yourself. If you haven't figured out yet what your stakes and lines are, no one else will know them either.

Authentic people are known for standing alone when they have to; some are willing to risk their safety or even their lives to defend a principle they believe to be imperative. While you have most likely not been faced with a life-or-death scenario in having to defend a value you hold dear, you are certainly inspired by those who have. For example, recently the world has been focused on the merits and courage of Malala Yousafzai, the Pakistani teenager who was shot in the head for being an outspoken advocate for the rights of girls in her country to be educated. Fortunately, she survived the cowardly attempt on her life. What has gripped the world is how this young person is so clear and dedicated to something bigger than herself, willing to back what she believes at the risk of her own personal safety. That truly is the ultimate test of a person's conviction.

Authentic people are known for standing alone when they have to; some are willing to risk their safety or even their lives to defend a principle or value they believe to be imperative.

DOES AUTHENTIC LEADERSHIP REALLY MATTER?

It matters that you're trustworthy when one of your peers is having a difficult time with a customer and has been reluctant to ask anyone for advice or support, but now she's wandered into your office with something clearly on her mind. There's a reason why she's come to see you.

It matters that you're switched on when a member of the budget working group attempts to sway your vote in advance of an important meeting. For him, the upcoming budget battle is about holding ground and preserving turf. You challenge him to go into the meeting wearing a different mindset — how the company wins. There's a reason why he's pondering your words with curiosity.

It matters that you're genuinely interested in others when one of your direct reports feels the pressure to see a special project he's leading through to launch next month, even while his mother is dying thousands of miles away. You ask him to reflect on which will cause him the biggest regret on his own deathbed — having missed the launch or having missed one final moment with his mother. There's a reason why he's decided to take some time off.

It matters that you have the courage to be you when a younger member of staff comes to thank you for talking about a particular mistake you made earlier in your career, which made it possible for her to then do the same with her small team. There's a reason why your courage to be you resonated with her.

It matters that you exhibit flow and passion when the member of your team who couldn't fly in her last trimester of pregnancy, thereby missing the innovation awards ceremony at which your team has won top honours, learns that you've arranged to have her beamed in via Skype so that she can accept the award along with her peers. There's a reason why she and the team are overwhelmed with gratitude.

It matters that you walk the talk when you schedule a meeting with the CFO to point out some discrepancies in the discretionary spending policy, noting that it makes it harder for you to justify to your team a cut in their training budget while the executive team has just spent a lavish weekend in Fiji to farewell a retiring board director. There's a reason why the CFO has quietly started a review of executive perks.

It matters that you stand on values and principle when you call your salesperson with the longest tenure and strongest results in to tell him that his behaviours don't align with the company's value on workforce diversity. When he learns that there have been no complaints and yet you're taking this position with him anyway, there's a reason why he's no longer smiling.

In so many ways and for so many different reasons, authentic leadership really does matter, as does the fertile soil of vulnerability in which it grows. It's time now to dig into vulnerability.

AUTHENTIC LEADERSHIP

| Trustworthy | Switched on | Genuinely interested in others |

| Courage to be yourself | Exhibits flow and passion | Walks the talk |

Stands on values and principle

AUTHENTIC LEADERSHIP IS ROOTED IN VULNERABILITY

14.

Vulnerability: The wizard behind the curtain

Vulnerability is a scary word. A lot of people think of vulnerability as daunting in its magnitude and potential ramifications. We often hear about it in very big and very personal stories where people have been on the brink of making an important choice between 'safe' and 'not so safe'. Choosing 'safe' implies you weren't able to push through the wall of self-doubt, uncertainty and apprehension about failing or letting others down. And choosing 'not so safe' is often heralded as the next step in your personal journey toward courageous leadership. Yes, there will be the big moments and decision points in your life that really illuminate the choice of these two options. But the great majority of your encounters with vulnerability aren't in the spotlight at all. These encounters are called 'daily living', and you are probably more expert at it than you give yourself credit for.

SCENARIO

> You wake up to the alarm that you set for 6am. The night before, you decided that a 6am rise would give you about 30 minutes' prep time over breakfast before

leaving for work. You debated about setting the alarm for 5.30am, but you convinced yourself that you could re-read the report in 30 minutes. Besides, your partner hates it when the alarm goes off before 6am. You are surprised to see four new emails in your inbox this early, and you scan the subject lines quickly as you consider what you're going to wear. You choose the blue over the black; somehow blue feels right for today. The email from Sue is marked urgent, but Sue marks everything urgent, so you decide to wait until you get to work to open any of them. You have got to get your head across the report one more time before the meeting at nine. The hour's commute in will give you some time to sort through your approach. Too bad you didn't get a chance to run through the presentation with Mike. But you have made presentations with Mike a dozen times. You will be able to flow around each other with skill. You eat a light breakfast, largely ignoring your partner and two kids — who are largely ignoring you — and you make notes on the report. You mark a circle around one budget figure that stands out this morning for some particular reason. It hadn't occurred to you the day before that this figure seemed out of context, but this morning it does. And why hadn't Mike caught it either? Nothing you can do about it now; the reports have been distributed. As you kiss your partner goodbye, your mind is already two hours ahead and in the meeting room. You picture yourself explaining the discrepancy in the report. You wonder if that might come across as defensive if it's the very first thing you mention during the presentation. You decide they won't have a problem with that. Everyone around the table respects you and Mike. They'll surely cut you some slack for a minor error.

Now read this scenario again. How many times does this person encounter vulnerability while preparing to leave for work? If vulnerability is about big and scary choices, then it's unlikely that anything about this person's morning would qualify. If vulnerability is about the hundreds of choices you make to navigate your way through the quagmire of daily living, then you could probably relate to the person in the scenario. Not everything is buttoned down with perfect certainty and control, but there's something that enables you to move forward. Imagine the alternative — paralysis at every juncture, finally deciding to shut yourself off from the world, mitigating any risk of harm. A very small percentage of people, called agoraphobics, live in that space. The great majority of us are willing and able to move forward.

The point here is: vulnerability isn't the big green monster that lives under your bed, ready to pounce and smother you with anxiety and dread. It is more like the wizard behind the curtain in Oz, a mere mortal who can do very little harm to you once you strip away all the smoke and mirrors. For many people, vulnerability is a monster. And those who think they are impostors especially dread vulnerability, much like an agoraphobic dreads stepping outside the safety of home. Learning to put vulnerability in its proper perspective is the best thing you can do to beat Impostor Syndrome. Like Toto, the dog in Dorothy's Oz, you are the one who can expose the wizard behind the curtain for who he really is.

> Vulnerability is very much like breathing — so long as you're alive, they both just happen naturally. You can overthink breathing, just like you can overthink vulnerability. Just let yourself be. Breathe and be vulnerable. It's part of life . . . nothing more, nothing less.

WHAT THE CRITIC THINKS ABOUT VULNERABILITY

The Critic is somewhat sceptical of the notion that vulnerability is as natural as breathing. The Critic tends to be more on guard in anticipation of vulnerable moments, both small and large. Most days it is a full-time job filtering through the intricacies of daily living to root out the landmines that are waiting for you. But the Critic is skilled after years of coaching you, and understands that you shouldn't waste too much time fretting over which suit you will choose to wear to tonight's awards banquet. The conversation you will have with Mary tomorrow morning, when you tell her that you are removing her from the team, is definitely worth the fret. There will inevitably be consequences associated with that decision and you had better be ready for what's coming.

The Critic is more dignified and less harsh when in a proactive space, taking great pride and responsibility for encouraging you to minimise risk by being more cautious and conservative with your decisions. The Critic's strategy here is to contain vulnerability, accepting its inevitability, but hovering high enough above it to determine its parameters in your life. It is like defining the parameters of a caged lion: so long as you can keep it within its confines, everybody will remain safe — but it's probably best not to ever turn your back totally on vulnerability. The Critic believes that, like the caged lion, vulnerability never loses the instinct to pounce.

A.J.'S SITUATION

For A.J., the Critic's voice sounded eerily like her mother and, to a lesser extent, her grandmother. As was the case with these two women, the Critic was concerned that A.J. was opening herself up for unnecessary criticism by taking a job as a conference organiser. Why would someone nicknamed the 'human

tornado' set herself up for such scrutiny? And the
Critic would have been alive and well in A.J.'s ear
as she entered the conference on that first morning,
convincing her that it was in her best interests to inflate
both her name and title, and not to mention the size of
the company, to protect herself.

MICHELLE'S SITUATION

The Critic would have also been in Michelle Stanson's
ear in her early days with Nova, chastising her for
questioning her managers' best intentions to see
her become a general manager. It didn't matter that
Michelle was more energised by her initial role in IS
and that she had fancied herself as having particular
aptitude for information technology. The fact that
her superiors saw her as having management
potential should obviously take precedence over her
own aspiration, the Critic would have told her. *They
know what they are doing, and you don't want to run
the risk of seeming unknowledgeable or, even worse,
unappreciative.* As with the lion-keeper's situation, the
Critic's major advice to Michelle would be to keep the
vulnerability contained. And she has done just that,
even if that has meant keeping her own interests and
aspirations to herself.

DANIEL'S SITUATION

For Daniel, the Critic would have been in overdrive as
he was debating the decision to leave the prestigious
law firm, where he was on the path to partner, to join a
lesser-known company as a divisional HR director, a
role he had never been in before. To risk such exposure
— to open up such vast vulnerability — would have
provoked much chatter and consternation from the
Critic, even though Daniel would eventually decide to

pursue the new opportunity anyway. Daniel is unlike many people who eventually succumb to the Critic's expertise on the probability of failure, because the Critic's voice is most compelling when he is telling you why something can't happen: *The odds in favour of you being successful in the role are next to nil.* Daniel's biggest hope would be to prove the Critic wrong, especially knowing that the Critic is waiting for any opportunity to say 'I told you so'. *I told you it was a mistake, Daniel. You'll listen to me next time, won't you?*

PETER'S SITUATION

And for Peter, the Critic would have been an old friend whose counsel has been appreciated for years. 'Old heads' get to be old heads because they have generally played it safe, Peter would come to conclude. And the Critic would have been screaming in his ear when he came very close to telling the CEO that he didn't know the first thing about running such a huge P&L in one of their major growth markets. *You don't want to ask for help,* the Critic would have advised Peter. *Find a younger version of yourself to help you out when you get on the ground there in Brazil. Don't make things worse by suggesting you can't run the business.* Yes, the Critic would have been in serious containment mode with Peter's vulnerability on that fateful day when he learned he was being sent to Brazil. He hadn't seen this one coming, so he would have to move into some serious damage control before his reputation was sullied. *Zip it up and say very little,* Peter's Critic would tell him repeatedly once he was on the ground in São Paulo.

It's worth repeating that the Critic loves you, and is therefore suspicious of any vulnerability, small or large, that might catch you off guard. As ironic as it seems, the Critic considers his ability to predict and control vulnerability as one of the major roles he plays for you. The Critic hasn't quite worked it out that the very essence of vulnerability is to live free outside the cage, rather than within. *There is way too much risk inherent in this approach to life,* the Critic will advise you. After all, the Critic loves you too much to ever see you hurt while under his careful watch and scrutiny.

WHAT THE COACH THINKS ABOUT VULNERABILITY

As you can imagine, the Coach has a different relationship with vulnerability than the Critic does. The Coach and vulnerability know each other well, with mutual admiration and respect. The Coach doesn't consider vulnerability as something to be contained or caged. Such a frame would reinforce the idea that vulnerability is dangerous and sinister, and the very idea works against the Coach's preference to use vulnerability rather than fear it.

The Coach likes to see you stretched rather than complacent. The Coach gets most concerned when you are too comfortable, which is a point of paradox for a lot of successful people. Comfort may work against you if there is no stretch inherent in most of your day-to-day challenges and encounters. So the Coach sees vulnerability as fuel for stretch — something you walk eagerly toward rather than something to be avoided at all costs. And, in the interest of making you more capable, the Coach is constantly scanning for opportunities to stretch and grow you, to take you outside your comfort zone, to push you to a new level of performance. Whereas the Critic is scanning for vulnerability to contain it, the Coach is scanning for vulnerability to *use* it.

A.J.'S SITUATION

The Coach would have been a big fan of A.J. and her spunk and determination as a teenager, applauding her for rejecting the safety of a sheltered existence and resisting pressure to go directly from high school to university. The Coach would have helped A.J. use her vulnerability as fuel for action, sparking her decision to leave home and start her adult life in Timaru, working the odd jobs until she landed a job with Blue Ridge. And the Coach would have been particularly proud of A.J.'s decision to do something that she had no experience with, but trusted in herself to get in there and start climbing the learning curve.

MICHELLE'S SITUATION

In Michelle's case, the Coach would have been in her ear when her parents and teachers began to discover her strong learning aptitude at a very early age. Being the youngest competitor in a lot of events might have seemed daunting for most kids, but Michelle took it all in her stride, liking the energy it gave her, not knowing at the time that this energy was called 'confidence'. By the time she was a teenager considering university options, being stretched had become a part of Michelle's persona, although she would discover later in life that it was far better to be the one initiating it herself. Vulnerability intensifies when others bring stretch to you, which was certainly the case with Michelle's promotion to be on the Australian team. The Coach would have been encouraging Michelle to rely on previous lessons to build an action plan and go for it. Like many people, Michelle sometimes wonders whether the Coach is too much of an optimist. After all, she is the one on the front line having to deal with the consequences of her actions.

DANIEL'S SITUATION

Daniel could relate to that sentiment as well, even

though he was far more used to initiating stretch in his own life than had been the case with Michelle. 'Going off the beaten track' had become something Daniel was known for and proud of. He saw this mantra as part of his personal brand, which he believed defined his attitude toward risk. Daniel liked being a risk-taker, and the Coach liked that Daniel was receptive to his encouragement. What Daniel didn't anticipate was his own over-reaction to the decision to deviate from the predictable and certain path to partnership. He had always dealt well in this space of vulnerability, especially when self-initiated. Now he wondered if he had gone too far this time. He could hear the Coach rooting for him, and he found himself needing every bit of that encouragement as he tried to adapt to his new role.

PETER'S SITUATION

For Peter, the Coach was an old friend and trusted adviser. That relationship had certainly come to light during Raewyn's recuperation from breast cancer. Peter found that the optimistic voice of the Coach in his own ear had helped him mirror the same for Raewyn, who also seemed to appreciate the energy that comes with being told what you can do, not what you can't. And even while facing a surge of self-doubt stemming from what felt like a loss of control over his destiny, Peter found himself drawn to his new boss in much the same way as he was drawn to the Coach. Both normalised his fear and helped him put vulnerability in proper perspective. With the right support around him, Peter was convinced he would be able to handle the challenge of Brazil.

Breathing and vulnerability — the Coach understands and appreciates the analogy far better than the Critic ever will. It most certainly has something to do with optimism and the ability to just let go and let things be. Some people call this faith. The need to predict and control every outcome runs counter to the need to purposefully impose stretch — and uncertainty — into one's life. At their extremes, these two frames cannot co-exist in harmony. The Coach does everything he can to convince you that choosing vulnerability is the healthier option.

THE WOMAN WITH PURPLE HAIR

This is a story about a woman with purple in her hair. For the purposes of this story, let's call her Tina. The real Tina exists, and I am taking liberty to tell her story here because I believe it captures the essence of the true antidote to Impostor Syndrome. While Tina's story may be about purple hair, you will see parallels to yourself and many people you know, love and work with.

Tina was 26 years old when I met her. She was an analyst who worked in corporate finance, and she worked on a variety of business projects, some of them in their incubator phase and requiring the support of people like her. Like many of her analyst peers, Tina worked inordinate hours, often on weekends too. They moved from one board paper deadline to the next, scanning through tons of research and competitor reports, and glued to their phones and emails to see what revisions needed to be made or what new information could be added.

Like her peers, Tina was selected for the role right out of university because she showed 'high potential' and great promise. And like her peers, Tina had no idea what that really meant, but she liked the attention it afforded her, and, more importantly, the exciting projects she had a chance to work on. A side benefit was the opportunity to travel occasionally. Tina's favourite trip had been to the company's business unit in Japan. She stayed an entire week longer and took a detour into the heartland of Japan to immerse herself in a country and culture that intrigued her. Whereas some would have found the prospect of backpacking alone in the countryside of Japan a bit frightening, this was right up Tina's alley. She had never really been afraid of adventure. For many reasons, the job felt right to her, and she received very positive feedback from client groups who found her insights and recommendations top-notch.

Then one day, Tina showed up to work with a shock of brilliant purple through her long brown hair. The purple blast of colour was pronounced, certainly not subtle. It was different. It was distinct. It was most definitely unique, especially in that department and in that company. There was nothing else different about Tina on this particular day. She was dressed in her usual business casual attire, neatly pressed blouse and pants, a smart jacket to match. Tina's father had been a cop and he had always stressed the importance of well-polished shoes. He would have been proud of his daughter's shoes on this day — they were sparkling. But no one was interested in Tina's shoes on that particular day. Her purple hair was what people from other floors were creating excuses to come and see.

A week later, Tina's manager asked me if I might consider meeting with Tina, to get to know her better, but also to perhaps offer some coaching related to her 'presence'. The manager clearly thought that Tina was lacking presence, and therefore was less influential than she might be. In my role, it was certainly not an unusual request for me to meet with the company's future leaders. I probed the manager for some context and learned that these concerns about Tina were rather recent, and were not indicative of her ability over the previous two years. While the manager couldn't attribute Tina's sudden lack of influence to anything specific, he danced around the subject of image, using the word 'eccentric' at one point to describe her. I knew then that this was about the purple hair. Tina's hair had become the elephant in the room. Except the proverbial elephant, which many people consider to be pink, was very, very purple.

A few days later Tina came to see me, and she was particularly animated during our conversation. You could tell something had created an energy in her that was hard to describe, but it seemed to convey a mix of consternation and fortitude. Underneath that very strong persona, I sensed Tina needed to talk. And we did, for nearly an hour. And the conversation was one I will never forget and one I have wished a dozen times I could do over.

Tina talked about her purple hair. I got to see it up close and personal, right there in the spotlight, for nearly an hour, just me and Tina. She talked about how her life had changed since that fateful weekend she had spent with her two sisters, both older, and both co-conspirators in the decision that all three had made: to put a streak of purple colour in their hair and see who could keep it in the longest. However, what had started out as a playful dare had become an existential crisis for this 26-year-old woman. She was not about to lose a bet with her two larger-than-life sisters, but nonetheless she had become

> **What had started out as a playful dare had become an existential crisis. Tina described it as feeling suddenly like an outsider . . . having to work extra hard to get in.**

increasingly aware that the purple streak in her hair was causing an unusual dynamic among the team. Tina described it as feeling suddenly like an outsider. Over the previous 10 days she had felt as though she was standing on the outside of a circle, having to work extra hard to get in. That had not been her experience previously. Tina was a smart woman. She knew she had unknowingly put herself in the middle of some grand experiment where the outcome seemed to be about some kind of reconciliation. Those weren't Tina's words, but rather my own after years of reflection on this wonderful conversation.

She felt isolated but she had nearly convinced herself that it was all in her imagination, until one of her peers strongly urged her to take out the purple dye. Tina hadn't been proud of the way she reacted, wishing she could have answered with a more polished response. She told her peers: 'I'm making a new fashion statement around here.' Obviously that hadn't gone down particularly well on the floor, with Tina sensing more and more the feeling of having to work extra hard to get into the circle. Her goal hadn't been to make a new fashion statement. Her goal had been to not lose a silly bet with her silly sisters, but now she found herself the protector of all things purple! Tina told me that, for the first time in her life, she was the outsider trying to get in and she felt an incredible urge to hold her ground. This had become a 'stake in the ground' moment for Tina. She would never have predicted a month earlier that she would be defending the right to have purple hair.

I learned a lot about Tina in that hour, and I was especially proud that she worked for us. She was smart, personable, intuitive, and an eager learner. What I don't think she appreciated on that day was how important her dilemma was, not just to her, but to others who have also found themselves defending their own version of purple hair. Tina knew that she had been sent to see me because her hair was purple. She asked me point-blank: 'Should I take it out?' I didn't tell her to colour over the purple, but I didn't tell her not to. My soul was screaming 'Keep it in!', but my corporate self kept me in check. So in the end I advised Tina that the ability to influence is about showing good judgement, and she would ultimately decide what was best.

With one week to go in her dare with her sisters, I thought Tina's dilemma would soon be over anyway. What I didn't realise, and nor did Tina, was that she was in the eye of the storm — a very personal, defining moment in a calibration of character — that would prompt her to walk in two weeks later, the purple in her hair beginning to fade, and resign.

RECONCILIATION

I said earlier that I wish I could rewind the hands of time back to that meeting with Tina, right at the point where she asked my advice on what she should do. Hindsight is truly a keen beast. I have had years to reflect on that conversation with Tina, and I have grown to appreciate that she would have been in the middle of an incredible tug-of-war between who she was and who others wanted her to be. It wasn't really about the purple hair — in retrospect, that was the tip of an iceberg that ran much deeper into the roots of the company's culture. The purple hair was a convenient distraction to divert attention away from the larger and more important issue at hand.

What Tina taught me, more than anything else, was that the tug-of-war is a constant calibration between standing out and fitting in. And that space in the middle of the tug-of-war is where vulnerability lives. It is that space in the middle, the line neither side is willing to be pulled across, that truly describes what a person feels in the midst of vulnerability. Stand out or fit in. Wear the bold red tie or go with the standard blue. Stand out or fit in. Disagree with the boss or keep it to yourself. Stand out or fit in. Tell your peers to knock off the sexual jokes about the new member of staff or join in. Stand out or fit in. Open the presentation with a story or open with PowerPoint. Stand out or fit in. Keep in the purple or wash it out. Stand out or fit in.

WHO I AM   WHO OTHERS WANT ME TO BE

It turned out that Tina's reckoning moment with vulnerability opened my eyes to the reality of the dozens of times each day we play tug-of-war — the quagmire of daily living. Vulnerability is not some terrible monster. It's not the great and powerful Wizard of Oz. Vulnerability is the true essence of daily living. Like breathing, we move toward vulnerability without conscious forethought, but become more aware of it when the tension mounts between standing out or fitting in. Plug in whatever words work for you. Taking a risk or playing it safe. Possibility or probability. Exuberance or caution. Loud or reserved. Liberal or conservative. Leading from the front or leading from behind.

And, yes, listening to the Critic or to the Coach. There's a space in between each of these extremes. Each time you get pulled near that space, you calibrate once more around 'who I am' and 'who others want me to be'.

WHO I AM WHO OTHERS WANT ME TO BE

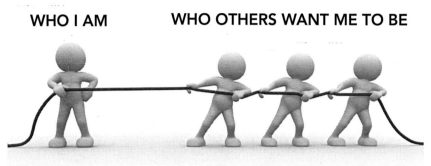

VULNERABILITY

That is what reconciliation is all about. In the tug-of-war between yourself and daily living, it is about restoring harmony, understanding that neither extreme is optimal in a world that thrives on interdependence. Had Tina switched to orange hair to make an even bolder point, she would have lost all influence, rendering her ineffective. Had she succumbed to the implicit norm that only certain styles are acceptable, she would have struggled intensely with her integrity. Even as the controversial purple faded from her hair, Tina ultimately sided with her personal sense of integrity, deciding she wouldn't work for a company that she believed made it difficult to express individuality.

The symptoms of Impostor Syndrome flare up the most when the tug-of-war intensifies between 'who I am' and 'who others want me to be'. Unless you can reconcile the tension, you are more than likely to experience a full outbreak of Impostor Syndrome — mask and all. Others may be pleased with your willingness to play the game by their rules, but they are not getting the full energy that you might bring if you didn't have to disengage from who you are.

Disengaging from who you are to become who others want you to be is like hanging your true personality on a coat rack every time you walk into work. It's as simple as that. You walk through the door, hang who you are on the coat rack and you reach for the impostor's mask so you can live up to who others want you to be. And then you take the impostor's mask off at the end of the day, drop it in the box near the door, and put on your personality again before walking out to start your evening. Think about going through that routine, day in and day out.

THE FOUR PROFILE SITUATIONS

For A.J., the tug-of-war was about maintaining her zest and energy in the face of criticism that these were liabilities. For Michelle, it was sorting out whether her aspirations were truly her own. Daniel's tug-of-war had to do with relaxing his pride and asking for help without losing face. And in his quest to help the company mitigate reputational risk, Peter's battle was to not lose sight of what so many others had come to love about him. Each of them would have to find, and become comfortable in, that middle ground known as vulnerability. For that is where authenticity resides.

15.

Beating Impostor Syndrome

If the symptoms of Impostor Syndrome are most likely to surface when you open yourself to vulnerability, you will want to consider the following strategies to recognise and minimise the symptoms' impact. Take note that these strategies are embedded in frames that may be new for you. You have to give yourself some time to lock in these new frames.

IMPERFECTION IS THE NORM

While perfection is a noble goal, we live in an imperfect world and our own imperfection helps us fit and connect. Imperfection is not an excuse, but simply a reality that helps you calibrate your starting point. You are more likely to be successful if you are honest with yourself about those things you don't do well, and may never do well. You can also take a lot of pressure off yourself by helping others understand that you are never going to be perfect. If you were perfect, why would you need them? And because you do need others in order to be successful yourself, give them a tangible handle on where they can help the most to counterbalance your imperfection. These are the connection points that create trust and a real sense of team.

THE RIGHT QUESTIONS LEAD TO THE BEST ANSWERS

There is an odd frame out there in the world that says the best leaders are the ones who have all the right answers. That would perhaps make life easier and simpler if your role was to always come up with the right answer. However, it might be far more valuable if you come up with the *question* that provokes the right discussion, which ultimately leads to the best answer. Let others find their way to the best answers through the important questions that you bring to the discussion. If everyone is racing toward the solution and no one has framed the right question, you may all end up in the wrong place. You can do something about that.

YOU CAN'T GROW WITHOUT PERSONAL STRETCH

It is virtually impossible to get from Point A to Point B without some degree of stretch — without some degree of rendering yourself vulnerable. It is important that you associate vulnerability with growth. What is even more important is that you prompt your own stretch on occasion, just to grow more resilient in the face of uncertainty and personal risk. Many people are passive with regard to their futures, preferring to position themselves as backseat drivers in their own lives, allowing others or luck to steer them toward the next destination. If you are proactive about your development and career progression, it means you are helping the organisation determine the path that will make you more capable over time.

GREY IS LARGER THAN BLACK AND WHITE

Ambiguity and uncertainty are far larger spaces than the narrower sphere of black-and-white certainty. And at its very core, leadership — at any level — is about your ability to disrupt the status quo in order to move to a different reality. When you are leading, you take yourself and others into that grey world where there aren't clearly paved paths to make the journey easy. You are often defining and paving those paths as you go, trusting your own instinct and intuition to serve you well in uncharted territory. Some refer to intuition as your sixth sense, and conventional wisdom suggests that women rely on it more explicitly than men do. Whatever you choose to call it, trust the internal radar that helps you navigate through the grey.

MOST PROBLEMS ARE MANAGED RATHER THAN SOLVED

If you consider many of the things you are dealing with at work (and in life), these aren't nice, neat issues that can be wrapped up in a little box with a pretty bow on top. Very few of our day-to-day challenges are problems that can be solved, never to surface again. You should consider most of your day-to-day challenges as polarities to manage rather than problems to solve. Many issues present in cycles; some predictably — like budget overruns, or forecasting shortfalls, or staff turnover. If you use the concept of the iceberg as a tool, you will discover that it is possible to break a negative cycle that you are in by changing the faulty frame that is driving it. That requires work, persistence and patience.

TURN UP THE VOLUME ON YOUR COACH'S VOICE

When Impostor Syndrome is in full swing, the volume on the Coach's voice is usually turned way down. The Critic may be quicker to the controls than the Coach, amplifying all the reasons why you should exercise prudent judgement and be very careful about moving into any grey area of uncertainty. That's when you should reach for the volume control and blast an injection of the Coach's optimism into your deliberation. Don't wait to call on the Coach until after vulnerability sets in, like you are waiting to be rescued. Seek out the Coach's voice earlier in your quest to stretch yourself, or when you are taking on a tall challenge and know you will benefit from a positive and encouraging voice. That voice can and should be your own.

KEEP YOUR CRITIC IN CHECK

Don't think that you can silence the Critic, as it is impossible to do and a waste of energy to try. And why should you? Remember, the Critic loves you and considers himself your guardian, scanning incessantly for anyone or anything that can harm you. Therefore, his voice gets louder as you venture away from the black-and-white world of certainty. Be mindful of both the Critic's volume and message when you increase your exposure to risk and uncertainty. The Critic will inevitably slow you down as he takes you through calculations to determine the probability of success. When the Critic is the loudest, your pessimism is likely to outweigh your optimism — so keep an ear open for when that balance needs adjusting.

FEEDBACK IS A GIFT

Kept in the right perspective, feedback from those you trust can help open your thinking about how to be a better person. Many of us associate feedback with personal pain, and rightfully so given how feedback is often used to correct rather than to reinforce. Moreover, for many of us feedback is something that happens to us, rather than something we actively seek. If leadership is about taking others with you, then some type of calibration is required occasionally to make sure people are tracking with you. Asking for feedback from those you trust can help you calibrate how well you are doing and help you identify what you might want to consider doing differently to get a better outcome. It is also a beautiful way to provoke vulnerability, another guaranteed way to build personal resilience.

APPRECIATE WHAT MAKES YOU UNIQUE

What is your fingerprint? How does it stand out from everyone around you, at home and at work, and in the outer limits of the world? Can you answer that question easily, or do you draw a blank? And is there something about you that not only makes you unique, but is a source of shame or humiliation? Unfortunately, others are often cruel or insensitive about those things you have little choice over, like race or gender or nationality. Or maybe even a prominent birthmark. We aren't born with an inclination to hide the things that define us as unique. We learn to hide the things that bring us scorn or ridicule or, in some cases, just the attention of others. As you consider your fingerprint, confront your decision to hide something about you that potentially can enhance your ability to influence and lead.

LEARN TO UNPLUG

Take off the make-up and let your hair down. Take off the tie and loosen your collar. Put on a pair of comfortable sweats, go for a walk through your neighbourhood, and look for reasons to stop and engage with others, or not. To be yourself, you have to know yourself. And that includes the good, the bad and the ugly. The unplugged you is the person whom those you trust the most are likely to see when you are not required to be 'on'. You have limits, you do get angry, and you do have the occasional bad day. These things don't make you inadequate; they merely make you human. If you trust that people will assume good intent in all you do, it gives you some latitude to be imperfect, especially when you are unplugged. That is when imperfection serves you in the best way possible, inspiring others to unplug as well.

16.

What companies can do about Impostor Syndrome

Company cultures often perpetuate the conditions that make it possible for Impostor Syndrome to thrive, sometimes at the deepest levels which are not obvious to the eye. There are implicit rules in every company that govern how employees conduct themselves. In some companies mistakes are not only acceptable, but are considered necessary in a culture that values innovation and risk-taking. In other organisations mistakes are frowned upon, and an individual can be tarnished by a single incident that might elsewhere be considered trivial. Hierarchical structures and codes of conduct are still alive and well in many companies, making it difficult for employees at the front line to have input into work processes and procedures that affect their work directly.

In companies where mistakes are not tolerated and risk-taking is viewed as the exception rather than the norm, those who are burdened by Impostor Syndrome will be especially careful to contain their worries. They will hide mistakes and refuse to ask for help or assistance out of fear of being perceived as a burden, or even worse, incompetent. And if individuality is discouraged and employees are expected to fit a particular mode of being, it becomes even more difficult for people to be their authentic selves, opting to fit in rather than stand out.

Leaders in companies can do something about Impostor Syndrome. It starts with an acknowledgement that no organisation, regardless of size, is immune from this common phenomenon. So long as there are people with high standards who are eager to succeed, be accepted and fit in, there will be inherent pressures to minimise risk and maximise safe options. Those are fertile conditions for someone who is wearing the impostor's mask inside an organisation. Taking less risk means there is less chance of standing out — just what impostors prefer.

Impostor Syndrome is not just something that has a fancy name — you can actually do something about it.

The strategies listed below are actions that companies can take to make it acceptable for employees at all levels to be better learners, a prerequisite to being better leaders. You can take a proactive stance in creating an environment where authentic leadership really does matter. Impostor Syndrome is not just something that has a fancy name — you can actually do something about it.

INVEST IN STRETCH

Many companies put little, if any, forethought into how they stretch and grow employees to greater levels of capability and competence. In fact, most companies do 'stretch' poorly, and in some cases perpetuate Impostor Syndrome by making it unacceptable for their rising stars to show vulnerability at a critical time when it is quite normal for them to experience it. I have come across some senior leaders who believe that a true test of a person's potential to lead is to throw them in the deep end and see how they fare. While there is definitely some merit to testing future leaders under pressure, it can become a costly venture when you put an important project or part of the business at risk, not to mention the likelihood that you will lose a talented person who de-rails as a result of inadequate support.

There is also a prevalent mindset that successful stretch is mostly about people being able to find their own way, sometimes with little or no forethought from the managers who are responsible for tracking their progress. Most managers who are trying to lift an employee's capability are likely to be operating largely off intuition driven by their own personal experiences. There are tools now that can help guide us on things like determining a person's aptitude or readiness for a new or different role, or assessing whether a person's learning or change agility is compatible with the demands or constraints of a challenging assignment. And we know far more about the precipitants of career de-railment than we did two decades ago. Yet most managers today aren't familiar with some of the basics associated with successful stretch. This is an area that companies need to pay more attention to and invest in training, not only for those being stretched, but for those doing the stretching.

DEMYSTIFY 'POTENTIAL'

The word 'potential' has been the source of much consternation and debate in companies, often with the unanticipated consequence of leaving some employees demotivated and turned off to the prospect of advancement. The traditional talent and succession-planning matrices often call for an assessment of employees' potential, which can determine how much a company is willing to invest in any person's growth and development. When you rank people as 'high potential', it implies that others have 'low potential' — and what a horrific stigma to attach to people who come to work each day trying to make a difference.

It is far better to talk about a person's *span* rather than their potential, as it speaks to the appetite employees may have to venture beyond the realm of technical expertise into the broader realm of management or cross-functional roles. Span is about the direction of travel for career progression, with lower span implying greater investment in technical training, and higher span implying greater investment in management training. Regardless of how you classify a person in terms of their span, it is clear their ongoing development is a priority. When you classify people on their potential, you inevitably end up with the unintended consequence of many people feeling devalued. In this case, semantics makes a huge difference.

VALIDATE THAT LEADERSHIP REQUIRES DISRUPTION

The old adage 'be careful what you pray for' applies to companies that say they value strong leadership, innovation and risk-taking. All of the above imply a tolerance for disruption, particularly if the status quo is considered the biggest impediment to growth. Leadership is about taking people to a different place. It is hard to navigate and lead that journey without first disrupting aspects of the current reality. And it is hard to disrupt anything without making some degree of noise. When we tell our leaders that we want them to drive change, but then we signal to them that they have to do so with little or no noise, we are sending a mixed and contradictory message. If anything, you should be more concerned if there is no noise associated with change. In the absence of noise, people may have not yet realised that they are supposed to be doing things differently.

One of the symptoms of Impostor Syndrome is to minimise the noise around you, to detract attention and focus away from yourself and onto something extraneous, particularly if things go wrong. When this happens, we miss the essence of a real learning opportunity. A part of taking risks and being innovative is to make the occasional mistake. Famous photographers take hundreds of photos to get that one perfect image. Success rarely happens without some missteps, so how can we make it okay and acceptable for our employees, particularly those in stretch, to make mistakes? And do so without expending more energy hiding those mistakes rather than discussing them? Disruption, noise, learning from mistakes — these are all attributes of leading change. What are the prevalent frames that define leadership in your company? Do those frames support disruption?

DETERMINE WHY LEADERSHIP AND AUTHENTICITY ARE IMPORTANT TOGETHER

Leaders who are comfortable being themselves make it easier for their teams to do the same. Leaders who put a premium on conformity make it difficult for their teams to deviate from these powerful norms. In turn, they stifle creativity, individual expressiveness and authenticity. The woman with purple hair, while she didn't intend to make a statement about her individuality, found that her acceptance by peers was largely a function of her willingness *not* to stand out. She found out, quite by accident and through a silly bet with her sisters, that her performance was largely assessed on the basis of her willingness to fit in. When she made the choice to stand out, her capability was questioned.

This is not to say that conformity isn't sometimes a valid if not noble objective. Women from Western cultures don traditional head scarves when working in Islamic cultures, largely out of respect for what is deemed acceptable and appropriate. You are more likely to influence successful outcomes if people see you as showing respect for what they think is important. There are many other examples of how conformity generates successful outcomes. The major point here is that companies must determine their own acceptance of individuality, knowing that you only get to test what the limits are when someone or some team pushes the boundary. If someone's individuality bothers you, the important question to ask is: Will my asking this person to conform make a material difference to the performance of the business, or will it just make me feel better? In many companies, conformity is not tied to business performance; it is tied to making managers feel better.

> **Companies must determine their own acceptance of individuality, knowing that you only get to test what the limits are when someone or some team pushes the boundary.**

SET THE EXAMPLE IN THE EXECUTIVE SUITE

It starts at the very top. Chief executive or senior leaders who can acknowledge bouts with vulnerability and face-offs with those moments of reconciliation are powerful exemplars and role models for employees who want to make a real difference in the company. Many first-time CEOs (and those who remember their first CEO role) are very familiar with Impostor Syndrome. I have coached first-time chief executives who hadn't anticipated the pressures associated with everyone else's expectations that they be both omniscient and omnipotent. And if you decide to take on those expectations, you are more inclined to close yourself off from any scenarios which are likely to raise your sense of vulnerability — the very thing that makes you more compelling!

The symptoms are not just limited to CEOs, but are shared among those occupying board rooms and executive suites around the world. With greater roles and titles come greater responsibilities, and, almost without fail, greater expectations. In those who have been around the longest, you will often find the biggest struggles with the Critic, who insists that their success must beget further success, all the while minimising as many 'vulnerability encounters' as possible.

CREATE VULNERABILITY ENCOUNTERS

There is a distinct difference between dialogue and debate. The former is about divergence and exploration. The latter is about convergence and decision. These are two different ways that leaders can engage with others to improve the quality of thinking and decision-making. Vulnerability can happen in either of these spaces, as the zones of dialogue and debate are often viewed as natural preferences. Taking people out of their comfort zones in terms of how they prefer to lead others will create vulnerability encounters. The more you encounter vulnerability, the less of a stranger it becomes.

Vulnerability encounters come in all shapes and sizes, but they have one thing in common: they create opportunities for people to step away from absolute certainty and safety, to venture into uncertainty and risky territory, and to rely on the elements of who they are to drive them toward successful outcomes. A politician who answers a question with 'I don't know'. A rugby player who decides within a millisecond to take a kick for goal, rather than pass the ball. An aspiring actor who decides to try her hand at improv. A church minister who must comfort a bereaved parent. These are all vulnerability encounters. And they all pull us away from a place of safety and toward a space where our leadership might make a huge difference.

NORMALISE THE SYNDROME

People new to a company experience it. People promoted into bigger roles experience it. People who stand out, or are singled out, for being different experience it. Young people experience it. Older people experience it. The novice apprentice and the newly appointed chief executive experience it. Most people who walk through the door each morning have experienced it. It is hard to believe that something that is experienced by most people is also something that most people are reluctant to acknowledge or talk about. Impostor Syndrome. Like any commodity, it's not so big and bad when everybody else has experienced it too!

Impostor Syndrome isn't new. It is as common as . . . well, the common cold. And just like the common cold, you can treat the symptoms of Impostor Syndrome, or you can make some fundamental changes that will decrease its recurrence across time. You should consider yourself fortunate to have that choice.

Make the choice to stretch yourself and, just as importantly, to serve as a coach or mentor to someone else who wants to grow and flourish as an authentic person. How cool is that?

17.

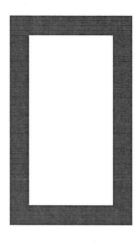

The final frame

To write this final frame for *The Impostor Syndrome*, I decided to spend a weekend on Waiheke Island, a 45-minute ferry excursion from Auckland. I had come to Waiheke Island two months earlier to re-write the section on frames. At that time, I found the air and atmosphere to be conducive to deep personal reflection, which helped me to get into flow when I needed it the most. So I wanted to replicate that earlier experience, as I needed to bring it all home in a final page.

I got off the ferry at Waiheke and walked through the terminal and out to the street to take a taxi to the villa where I was staying for the weekend. There were many taxis parked along the curb, and one driver pointed me to one of his mates across the street, who ended up being my driver. I never got his name, but I learned that his family moved from the United Kingdom to New Zealand and Waiheke Island in 1954 when he was four years old. He had lived on the island since the middle of the last century, and he had mapped the progression of time against some personal markers that I found quite fascinating. He had been a volunteer fireman in his early years, and remembered having to take the fire-trucks over to Auckland by ferry for supplies and to refuel them. He had seen all the major roads put in and remembered the controversy associated with funding 'urban sprawl' on the island. He described the long-timers on Waiheke as 'traditionalists' and said he probably fit neatly into that category.

Halfway to the villa, he asked me why I had come to Waiheke for the weekend. I told him I was there to write the closing to a book. He asked me what the book was about. I told him it was called *The Impostor Syndrome* and told him a little about the major premise. I told him the book was about people who put pressure on themselves to be perfect, making it more difficult for them to just be themselves.

And here comes the reason why I am telling you this story as the final frame. The driver shrugged his shoulders and said to me, 'Well, that sounds like a whole lot of work, trying to be somebody you aren't. Seems to me it would be a whole lot easier just to be who you are.'

I told him I agreed with him. And then he asked, 'Why would you want to work harder than you have to?' He continued, 'That doesn't make any sense.'

Again, I told him I agreed with him. To which he asked, 'Do you really work with a lot of people who spend most of their time trying to be somebody else?' And before I could answer, he said, 'I don't get that.'

I'd like to thank the driver, who works for Island Taxis, for helping to put the whole book into context and for helping me write the final frame even before we arrived at the villa. Turns out he made my weekend a very enjoyable one. The simplicity and genuineness of his words gave me pause for deep personal reflection about one of life's more compelling paradoxes. It *is* hard to know why we work harder than we have to just to feel okay about ourselves. The truth is that less really *is* more. The less you pressure yourself to be perfect, the more you are able to give of yourself in a way that really does make a difference.

Go ahead and try it. Lose the mask and unplug.

18.

Finding your fingerprint

The activities that follow are designed to help you explore facets of your being that distinguish you as unique. You can also use these exercises when you are coaching or mentoring others. It is important that you are clear about who you are, who you are not, and what you are ultimately about in order to live your life to the fullest and be able to offer all you are capable of. Once you have thought through and identified 'who you are', you can translate this knowledge to the frames you have in your life, and explore whether they are enabling you or impeding your growth.

Spend some time exploring the authentic you. And always remember: there has only ever been, and will always only be, one you. Would you dare deprive the world of that gift?

'SO, TELL ME ABOUT YOURSELF'

At professional and social gatherings, it is not unusual for someone to say to you, 'So, tell me about yourself.' You probably get the opportunity to introduce yourself, formally or informally, hundreds of times in a given year. In most of these situations, it is another person's or group's initial exposure to you. With these opportunities to introduce yourself to others, how much do you really reveal about who you truly are? And in the past, how many times have you given in to the temptation to answer that question as safely as you possibly can? As you might imagine, an impostor hates being asked to answer that question.

In a professional or work context, people are far more inclined to define themselves by virtue of what they do rather than who they are. That is why it is not surprising that work colleagues often know very little about each other beyond the professional realm. Even in social scenarios, you are often inclined to define yourself by what you do rather than who you are. Often the safest and most comfortable way to break the ice with someone new is to focus on the 'what' rather than the 'who'. While both the what and the who are important, there is a tendency to gravitate toward the former if you are uncomfortable or uncertain about the latter. Keep this distinction in mind as you consider your own authenticity.

WHO I AM

These are the attributes of your persona, much like the whorls and ridges in your fingerprint. What you write here should capture the essence of you, the person.

_____

_____

_____

_____

WHAT I DO

These are the activities that occupy the majority of your time, professionally and/or personally. Others may infer certain attributes about your persona based on these activities.

_____

_____

_____

_____

ANALYSIS

Now compare what you have written. Is there more congruence or discrepancy between who you are and what you do? What frames would you have to modify in order to create more overlap between the two?

_____

_____

_____

_____

_____

_____

_____

_____

_____

_____

_____

_____

_____

_____

_____

_____

EXAMPLE

Who I am	I am the third son of John and Sharon, the brother of David and Conor, the husband of Siobhan, the father of Ben and Corey, the best friend of Dan, the manager of my team. I am a part of many important relationships.
What I do	At this stage of my life, I spend most of my time at work, even when I'm at home. I'm an engineer, so my head is constantly in that space. I have routines that define my day and week, especially my weekend. Except for the occasional nap, my life feels pretty regimented.
Analysis	I define myself in terms of important relationships, but I don't really make the time for them, other than perhaps my team. All of these relationships are sources of energy for me, but they clearly aren't a priority. My work life is clearly the priority right now. I'm not sure I like writing that. I've got a major frame to change.

THREE WORDS

According to the most recent edition of the *Oxford English Dictionary*, there are a quarter of a million distinct English words, of which half are nouns, one-quarter adjectives and one-seventh verbs. Any of these words may serve to paint a picture of who you are. Of the thousands of possible choices of words to describe yourself, let's see if you can narrow it down to three.

WHY ONLY THREE?

This 'three words' exercise is important for three reasons. First, it makes you consciously aware that you play a vital role in shaping how others perceive you — whether that be a narrow slice or a broad purview of you, the person. You only get one chance to make a first (and often lasting) impression, so you will want to be more deliberate about how you want other people to experience you. Taking yourself through a deliberate process of finding three words that best define 'you' will be both challenging and revealing.

Secondly, you get a chance to see if there is a correlation between the three words you use to define yourself and the energy you derive from 'being' those words. When you consider the sum effect across the three words that you choose, does the composite energise or drain you? For example, defining your work role as 'manager' might make you feel the weight of responsibility, whereas 'leader' might make you feel inspired and strong.

Lastly, this exercise gives you an opportunity to assess how comfortable you are with being unique. If authenticity is about embracing what makes you unique, you have to have a starting point. This might mean dragging yourself out of the shadows or seeking to be more precise — adopting 'free-thinker' rather than 'liberal', for instance.

STEP 1: PERSONAL REFLECTION

Before choosing words that describe who you are, it will be important to scroll through memories of important and defining moments in your life, through people and experiences that have stretched and tested you under both optimal and adverse circumstances. If you consider your life as a journey, and yourself as an evolving product of that journey, you should think carefully about words that shed the most light on who you truly are.

STEP 2: 26 WORDS

With a dictionary in hand or online, make your way quickly through the pages of the 26 letters in the alphabet. Scroll through at a reasonably fast pace and let your eye pause where it is drawn to, for whatever reason. For each letter of the alphabet, you can choose only one word that best describes who you are. Put the 26 words on one page, but mix them up so that they aren't in alphabetical order.

1. _____
2. _____
3. _____
4. _____
5. _____
6. _____
7. _____
8. _____
9. _____
10. _____
11. _____
12. _____
13. _____
14. _____
15. _____
16. _____

17. _____
18. _____
19. _____
20. _____
21. _____
22. _____
23. _____
24. _____
25. _____
26. _____

STEP 3: 13 WORDS

With your list of 26 words in front of you, put a circle around the top 13 words that *best* describe who you are. You are now making some deliberate choices. The 13 words you have circled have now become your new list.

1. _____
2. _____
3. _____
4. _____
5. _____
6. _____
7. _____
8. _____
9. _____
10. _____
11. _____
12. _____
13. _____

STEP 4: REALITY CHECK

Send your list of 13 words to two people in your life who know you the best and are not afraid to be candid and genuine with you. These two people may include your partner, a parent, sibling, friend or mentor.

Ask these two people to put a cross next to any of the 13 words that *don't* match their perception of who you are. They don't have to justify or explain any of their choices. It's okay if they agree with all of your 13 words. It's okay if they don't agree with any of them.

STEP 5: SEVEN WORDS

After some deep reflection on your list of 13 words *and* the input from the two people who know you best, now put a circle around the seven words that best define who you are. Once again, you are making some deliberate choices. It's okay if you choose words from the list that the other two people indicated are least like you. It may be that they are unaware of some things about yourself that you have not made explicit to them. It may be that you have spent some time and effort to make sure they don't see these things about you.

1. _____
2. _____
3. _____
4. _____
5. _____
6. _____
7. _____

STEP 6: FOUR DAYS, FOUR WORDS

For the next four days, choose one word each day to eliminate from your list of seven. By eliminating these four words, you are not saying that they don't describe who you are; you are simply saying that the three words remaining on your list are the ones that *best* describe who you are.

STEP 7: THREE WORDS

Write the three words on a clean sheet of paper. Under each word, write a few sentences about how the word applies to you. The example below may help you.

EXAMPLE	
Student	I have been a lifelong student, eager to learn new things about the world, and often challenging those around me to keep an open mind and not become enslaved by rigid frames. Being on a learning curve energises me. Being stretched energises me. If I always leave room for a better way, that means that possibility lives in infinity.
Destined	The spiritual side of me is fuelled by my belief that our lives are ordained, and, therefore, position us on particular paths at particular times to encounter particular people and experiences. I don't put much stock in coincidence or luck, as I consider those to be throwaway explanations for things that are meant to be and are meant for me.
Accountable	I am perplexed by anyone who walks away from a commitment, unashamedly leaving others to pick up the pieces. Accountability is a core value and it is strongest when felt from within rather than imposed from without. The opposite of feeling personal accountability for something is choosing to walk away with no ownership for the result if things start to unravel. I stand behind those things I commit to, even if they don't turn out the way I hope.

STEP 8: YOUR EPITAPH

> In loving memory of John Gray
> Husband, Father, Soldier

We usually don't get a choice of the epitaph inscribed on our tombstone. Let's assume you do get a choice.

   If a total stranger wandered up to your tombstone, are you comfortable with them deducing who you were as a person through the three words you have chosen in this exercise?

_____

_____

_____

1.   If not, what word(s) would you change? Why?

_____

_____

_____

2.   Does your epitaph say more about who you were or what you did?

_____

_____

_____

3.   Does that matter?

_____

_____

_____

4.   Does your epitaph define you as unique? Does the sum impact of the three words together truly capture the essence of your 'fingerprint'?

_____

_____

_____

5. If you could add a by-line at the bottom of the three words, what would it be? Consider this example.

    In loving memory of John Gray
    Husband, Father, Soldier
    'Born to Run'

What is your by-line?

_____

_____

_____

_____

_____

6. Looking at the three words and the by-line, choose one word to describe the essence of your epitaph.

_____

_____

_____

MY INHERENT GIFTS

Part of defining your uniqueness is to know something about your inherent gifts. A way of thinking about this is to ask yourself: 'In what way(s) am I gifted as a person?' A person's gifts are often referred to as their 'aptitude'. While most of our skills are learned, aptitude is considered to be an inherent predisposition to excel at certain things.

Some people are natural-born athletes. From early on, they have a gift at excelling in the physical realm, and they do so in a way that symbolises peak performance. Others are endowed with great musical ability, drawn to the energy associated with playing in a symphony orchestra or singing a solo on stage in front of thousands of people. Some people have what is called numeric aptitude, meaning they are particularly suited to roles or activities that require quantitative reasoning, not unusual for people who work in finance. Verbal aptitude is also considered a gift, most of us being able to think of a person we know who is exceptionally talented at articulating a vision in the written or spoken word and influencing others to follow. And then there are people who have what is known as diagrammatic aptitude, which means they have a natural gift at seeing systems. They tend to see patterns, relationships and interconnections in any challenge or opportunity they encounter. There are dozens of inherent gifts that manifest themselves in the people around us in our day-to-day encounters. It is difficult to find a person who isn't gifted in at least one particular realm.

Whether an inherent gift is manifested on a sports field or a theatre stage, in the workplace or a classroom, or even alone, it is important that you know what your gifts are, and that you assess your own comfort at having those gifts become a signature component of your uniqueness.

Following are the attributes of an inherent gift. Determine whether any or all of these attributes pertain to what you believe to be your gift.

AN INHERENT GIFT IS A SKILL OR ABILITY THAT:

- manifests fairly early in life, although is perhaps not fully realised until later in life
- may be driven largely by intuition or instinct, although it gets developed more fully through direct experience and learning
- perpetuates a heightened sense of confidence across time, enabling you to repeatedly lift your own personal success threshold
- you coach others on, formally or informally, and distinguishes you as a best practice or benchmark
- energises you and those who you choose to share it with
- classifies you in a league of your own, perhaps unique only to you
- others have recognised in you and have encouraged you to display.

Based on these attributes of an inherent gift, list what you believe to be your gift(s):

1. _____
2. _____
3. _____

Now list the three words from Activity 2:

1. _____
2. _____
3. _____

Now ask yourself whether the three words you have chosen to define who you are enable or provide some outlet to express your inherent gifts.

EXAMPLE

My three words to define who I am are:

Student, Destined, Accountable

My gifts are:

Patience, Empathy, Optimism

As a lifelong student, I like being on a learning curve, which is like being on a path that is stretching me. As I believe in destiny, I have to be patient not to get ahead of myself, possibly missing out on people and experiences along the way. I believe that patience and empathy are interlocked, slowing me down enough to appreciate what I am learning and allowing time to connect with others. My optimism serves as a personal source of energy, enabling everything about who I am. I like how my gifts have natural outlets through the three words that define who I am as a person.

How are you able to express your gifts through the confluence of words that define who you are? Write a couple of paragraphs that capture how 'who you are' enables or disables your gifts.

_____
_____
_____
_____
_____
_____
_____
_____
_____
_____
_____
_____

The Impostor Syndrome

MY FRAMES

Frames are mental constructs that you put around anything in order to give it meaning.

Think about the frames that you put around each of the following situations. First, write the words that best describe that particular frame. See the example on pages 152–53 for a completed exercise.

SITUATION	MY FRAME
When I succeed	

IS THIS FRAME:			
Mostly an enabler?		Mostly an impediment?	

SITUATION	MY FRAME
When I fail	

IS THIS FRAME:			
Mostly an enabler?		Mostly an impediment?	

SITUATION	MY FRAME
When I'm leading	

IS THIS FRAME:

Mostly an enabler?	Mostly an impediment?	

SITUATION	MY FRAME
When I am being led	

IS THIS FRAME:

Mostly an enabler?	Mostly an impediment?	

SITUATION	MY FRAME
When I am faced with uncertainty	

IS THIS FRAME:

Mostly an enabler?	Mostly an impediment?	

SITUATION	MY FRAME
When there is little risk	

IS THIS FRAME:

Mostly an enabler?	Mostly an impediment?	

SITUATION	MY FRAME
When someone disagrees with me	

IS THIS FRAME:

Mostly an enabler?		Mostly an impediment?	

SITUATION	MY FRAME
When someone else has a better idea	

IS THIS FRAME:

Mostly an enabler?		Mostly an impediment?	

SITUATION	MY FRAME
When someone else gets to decide	

IS THIS FRAME:

Mostly an enabler?		Mostly an impediment?	

SITUATION	MY FRAME
When I am unplugged	

IS THIS FRAME:

Mostly an enabler?		Mostly an impediment?	

For each situation listed above, review your frame. You have determined whether the frame is mostly an enabler or an impediment to your success. Now look at which frames you need to modify or alter significantly to make them enablers. Think about the symptoms discussed earlier in the book, and about what roles your Critic and Coach are playing: do their roles and your responses need to be modified? Are there other frames you employ which might benefit from this type of analysis and refining?

EXAMPLE

SITUATION	MY FRAME	
When I succeed	It's mostly about the team's success, not mine.	
IS THIS FRAME:		
Mostly an enabler?	Mostly an impediment?	X

WHAT DOES THIS TELL ME ABOUT MY ATTITUDE AND MINDSET?

I am not taking responsibility for my actions, but am hiding in the safety of the crowd. This means I can avoid responsibility when things go wrong, but also I can avoid the risk of failure involved in building on success and stretching myself to achieve more and improve my performance. Ultimately this is a passive approach and is not affirming or energising. The Critic's impulse to protect me against future harm or failure, even in the face of current success, is holding me back. The Coach's voice is drowned out by this fear and caution.

HOW CAN I REFRAME MY THINKING?

I can identify the role I individually play in the success. My communication skills and supportive nature make other team members feel safe to raise ideas and alternative options, and to take a lead and take responsibility in their core skill areas. By actively fostering a culture of collegiality, I make the team's effort greater than the sum of its parts. My Coach is telling me that this is something I can build on, perhaps by discussing with my boss new ways to push the project further.

MY DAYDREAMS

Daydreaming is as natural as thinking. In
fact, the mindless activity of daydreaming
occupies a lot of your consciousness
during the course of any given day.
Psychologists estimate that we daydream
for one-third to one-half of our waking
hours, although a single daydream lasts

only a few minutes. You might think of daydreaming as an outlet
— sort of like a decompressor for the mind when it is stretched
or strained or even lacking mental stimulation. Boredom, which is
considered a stressor, is a major catalyst for daydreaming.

In its most technical sense, daydreaming is a short-term
detachment from your immediate surroundings, during which you
create a visionary fantasy, typically filled with happy, pleasant thoughts,
hopes and ambitions, imagined as coming to pass — all while wide
awake! At their best, daydreams allow you a range of possibilities
which in the hard cold light of reality aren't likely to come to pass
without major transformation on your part. The beauty of daydreams
is that, in the particular moment, nothing is impossible. The dreams
are about what you can do and would like to do, not about imposing
constraints or restraints.

Specifically, daydreaming can help you cement your beliefs and
values, clearly important components to who you are as a person. For
example, when you daydream about scenarios in which you are trying
to convince someone of something you believe in strongly, you are
also in a sense getting to know yourself and what you stand for better.

For one workday week, record in the space below as many of
your daydreams as possible. Write down what you were doing in the
daydream and what the outcome was. At the end of the week, review
your daydream log and determine whether there are any prevalent
themes. What are you learning about yourself from your daydreams?
What do they tell you about either your current frustrations or future
aspirations?

DAYDREAM LOG

DAY 1	
DAY 2	
DAY 3	
DAY 4	
DAY 5	

FURTHER READING

The Age of Paradox by Charles Handy, Harvard Business Review Press, 1995

The Dance of Change by Peter Senge, Charlotte Roberts et al., Doubleday, 1999

The Fifth Discipline Fieldbook by Peter Senge, Charlotte Roberts et al., Doubleday, 1994

The Path of Least Resistance for Managers by Robert Fritz, Berrett-Koehler, 1999

True North: Discover Your Authentic Leadership by Bill George, Jossey-Bass, 2007

INDEX

ABOUT SIGMOID CURVE CONSULTING GROUP

The Sigmoid Curve Consulting Group specialises in tools and frameworks that enable leaders and their teams to navigate through the inevitable cycles of change. Rather than dealing with change in a reactive mode, teams build the capability to anticipate and proactively initiate change that enables the business to sustain growth and momentum. A fundamental premise that underlies our work is that leaders and teams have a choice about the relationship they establish with these cycles of change. You can either go through life as a back-seat passenger, or you can position yourself in the driver's seat, choosing the necessary turns and the speed at which you travel. Our tools and frameworks enable teams to make those choices wisely and with a collective sense of ownership and commitment to strong results.

Heavily influenced by the philosophy of what it takes to build a learning organisation, we believe there is a strong relationship between the respective capabilities to lead, learn and change. Effective leaders are effective learners; and effective learners are more adaptive to change. These three capabilities go hand-in-hand. Whether an individual leader or the team is focused on successful results, it all starts with the ability to ride the cycles of change, and be energised by what you're able to create when you truly understand the essence of the Sigmoid Curve.

For further information about the Sigmoid Curve Consulting Group, visit our website at www.sigmoidcurve.com